Canadian Pacific
Color Guide to Freight and Passenger Equipment

CP 504582, with Canadian Cancer Society trailer, Moose Jaw, Saskatchewan, September 3, 1983. *(Ronald A. Plazotta)*

John Riddell

Copyright © 1998
Morning Sun Books, Inc.

All rights reserved. This book may not be reproduced in part or in whole without written permission from the publisher, except in the case of brief quotations or reproductions of the cover for the purposes of review.

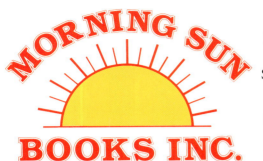

Published by
Morning Sun Books, Inc.
9 Pheasant Lane
Scotch Plains, NJ USA 07076

Library of Congress
Catalog Card No. 97-072728

First Printing
ISBN 1-878887-86-6

Color separation and printing by
The Kutztown Publishing Co., Inc.
Kutztown, Pennsylvania

Acknowledgements

This book has been accomplished with the support of many people.
The following photographers loaned slides that are included in the book:

Doug Cummings	W.J. McChesney	Lou Schmitz	Robert Turner
Emery Gulash	Don McQueen	Brian Schuff	Mike Wearing
Fred Headon	Jim McRae	Keith Sirman	Brian West
Tom Hood	Gary Ness	Bryan Sirman	Dave Whitall
Houser Collection	James O'Donnell	John Slean	Dale Wilson
Gordon Jomini	Jim Parker	David Stremes	Paul C. Winters
Ken Grist	Ronald Plazzotta	Graham Stremes	Gary Zuters

*My thanks to Jim Eager, Don McQueen and Dale Wilson for proofreading the photo captions.
In addition, the following people provided various information:* Ian Cranstone, Dale Wilson,
George Moore, Gordon Price of CP Rail, Peter Bowers, Al Westerfield, Gary Zuters.

*My thanks to Bob Yanosey of Morning Sun Books
for his support and assistance in the production of this Color Guide.*

Finally, all the captions were authored by myself and any mistakes are mine alone.

Canadian Pacific Table of Contents

Passenger Equipment		Freight Equipment	
Coaches	5	Boxcars	32
Combines	10	Refrigerator Cars	58
Sleeping Cars	11	Stock Cars	61
Dining/Restaurant Cars	14	Hoppers	65
Observation Cars	15	Covered Hoppers	69
CANADIAN Cars	17	Ore Cars	76
Head-End Cars	21	Gondolas	80
Official Cars	26	Flat Cars	91
		Cabooses	104
		Non-Revenue Equipment	115

Canadian Pacific
Color Guide to Freight and Passenger Equipment

Canadian Pacific Limited long advertised itself as 'The World's Most Complete Transportation System' with its rail (freight and passenger), steamships (cargo and passenger), airlines, trucking, express, hotels and telecommunications. Much has been written on many aspects of the fascinating Canadian Pacific Railway, however little has been published on its freight cars, passenger cars and maintenance-of-way rolling stock.

The purpose of this book is to provide an overview of this rolling stock in color photographs from 1940 to 1996. Much of the equipment shown was built years before color photography. No attempt has been made to cover all car types of the immense car fleet. The focus is to show typical equipment in normal paint and lettering, rather than the rare and unusual, however there are several exceptions. Little coverage is included of CP subsidiary lines such as the Grand River Railway, Quebec Central and Dominion Atlantic.

Roster size

As one of the largest railways in North America with some 34,600 km (or 21,500 miles) from Atlantic to Pacific, the Canadian Pacific has long had a large car fleet as shown in the following chart, which includes subsidiary lines:

	1902	1911	1929	1944	1955	1963	1981
Passenger	847	2,100	3,322	2,810	2,910	1,572	0
Freight	24,252	60,213	97,554	75,276	83,995	78,916	59,953
Non-revenue	1,122	2,559	5,623	4,030	5,593	5,129	5,075

Passenger cars were built by CP Shops (Angus, Hochelaga, Farnham, Perth), Canadian Car & Foundry, National Steel Car Company, Barney and Smith, Harlan & Hollingsworth, Ontario Car Co., Crossen Car Co., Pullman, Rhodes Curry and Ohio Falls Car Mfg Co. The stainless steel CANADIAN cars were built by the Budd Company in Philadelphia. On September 29, 1978, CP Rail transferred its passenger car fleet and services to the new Via Rail Canada.

The vast majority of freight cars were built by CP shops, Canadian Car & Foundry, National Steel Car and Eastern Car Co. In early years, several orders of freight cars were built in the U.S. by builders such as American Car & Foundry, Barney & Smith, Pressed Steel Car, Standard Steel Car Co., Western Car and Pullman. Boxcars for the International of Maine Division were built by Pullman-Standard in Indiana. CP built its cabooses in its own shops. While most rolling stock was purchased new, some equipment was acquired second-hand when CP leased or absorbed other railways, especially in earlier years.

Some types of freight cars were developed by the CP including high-side composite gondolas, 1929 radial-roof boxcars and bathtub gondolas. CP built the first dome cars for passenger train service in North America in 1902.

Columbus, Ohio, May 1967. *(Paul C. Winters)*

During the time era of the photos in this book, CP operated three major shops that built and repaired cars, in addition to diesel locomotive rebuilding, repairs and maintenance. Angus Shops was 200 acres in east-end of Montreal. At full capacity in 1937 it employed 8,000 men and could in one day build 10 new passenger cars, 15 new freight cars and complete 206 freight car repairs. Weston Shops was 284 acres in Winnipeg. At full capacity it employed 2,500 men. In each month, it repaired 40 passenger cars and 800 freight cars. Ogden Shops is 213 acres on the east side of Calgary. At full capacity it employed 1,200 men and repaired 500 freight cars per month. In earlier years, CP operated many other smaller car shops including: Hochelaga QC, Farnham QC, McAdam NB, Kentville NS, West Toronto ON, Perth ON, North Bay ON, Preston ON, Sherbrooke QC.

Format of captions

The caption of each photo includes a heading with the number of car pictured, the AAR classification code of car type and the car number series of the car. In many cases there were other series of identical or similar cars, so there were often many more similar cars than those of the specified series.

Numbering

Prior to 1913, CP assigned five-digit numbers to freight cars. Open-top cars received odd-only numbers while house cars received even-only numbers. In 1919 many car numbers were converted to six digits and consecutive numbering was used thenceforth for new cars. Non-revenue rolling stock used 'On Company Service' (OCS) is assigned 4xxxxx numbers. Like other Canadian railways, CP stamps each car's number in the steel sill on each side directly above the left truck. This allows the car number to be identified if the stencilled number is removed for any reason.

Montreal, June 17, 1979. *(Ronald Plazzotta)*

Paint/lettering schemes

From the earliest years, CP applied freight car red on enclosed cars such as boxcars, refrigerator cars, bunk cars and cabooses. Black was applied on open-top hoppers, covered hoppers, gondolas, flat cars, snow plows, spreaders and cranes.

Prior to 1947, freight equipment carried plain gothic 9" lettering CANADIAN PACIFIC. Starting in 1947 until 1951, the "Spans-the-World" logo was applied on box cars and reefers only. In 1951 CP started applying the stepped gothic CANADIAN PACIFIC RAILWAY lettering to boxcars and reefers.

In August 1962, CP started painting freight cars with CANADIAN PACIFIC in script lettering - first on new hoppers and gons and repainted box cars and reefers. The word RAILWAY was dropped to impress on the public that the numerous CP services including trucking, hotels, communications, lake and ocean shipping etc. were all part of one unified transportation system.

Approximately 1967, CP started painting its freight cars in different colors, with script lettering:

covered hoppers - *grey*
open hoppers - *black*
refrigerator cars -
 silver sides with red script, silver roof, black ends
insulated-heated boxcars -
 orange with red script, black ends, silver roofs
newsprint boxcars - *green sides, black ends, silver roofs*
cabooses - *bright red sides and yellow ends*
containers and trailers - *silver with red script*.

In June 1968, Canadian Pacific introduced a radical new corporate image for all aspects of the entire company including railway rolling stock. Freight cars were painted in different colors by type: 'Action Yellow' for cabooses and insulated cars; 'Action Green' for newsprint cars, 'Action Red' for boxcars, gondolas and flat cars; 'Action Silver' for refrigerator cars; black for hopper cars. With the new corporate image came a uniquely designed symbol called a "Multimark", consisting of a portion of a square, a circle segment and a triangle. The square represented corporate stability, the circle segment suggested global activities while the triangle denoted motion and movement. Chief executive officer, N.R. Crump, said "It clearly points to the future and implies that Canadian Pacific is constantly on the move." The Multimark of a red or black square in a white half-circle was painted on car sides, usually at the "B"-end. A 'symbol train' of two diesels and nine different freight cars in the bright new colors was unveiled to the public in Montreal on October 3, 1968. The train then made a cross-Canada tour stopping in Toronto, Sudbury, Fort William, Winnipeg, Regina, Moose Jaw, Swift Current, Medicine Hat, Calgary and Vancouver. In 1988, CP Rail stopped applying the Multimark when repainting freight cars.

CP stencils its freight cars with the appropriate A.A.R. classification code. Each photo caption includes the car's AAR class. CP also uses three-character codes to classify its car types but since these codes are used only for internal identification purposes and not stencilled on the cars, these CP codes are not referred to here.

Additional Reading

A large number of references were used in preparing the captions including various **Official Railway Equipment Registers (ORER)**, CP Equipment Summaries, CP Rail Equipment Data Book and **Canadian Trackside Guide**.

Numerous CP passenger cars, freight cars and MOW equipment are preserved across Canada. A detailed list is contained in the annual publication Canadian Trackside Guide.

Additional color photos of CP equipment can be found in the **Northern New England Color Guide** published by Morning Sun Books.

Columbus, Ohio, August 1967. *(Paul C. Winters)*

Passenger Cars

COACHES

CP 141 PA series 111-347
▲This is one of 236 65' wood suburban coaches, built in July 1907 by CP's Angus Shops. It is shown as restored for filming the 1973 television series **The National Dream** and carries 'CANADIAN PACIFIC RAILWAY' lettering and cornerpost ornamentation in gold leaf typical for CPR passenger cars in the 1880's, 20 years before this car was built. This car is preserved, painted as built in 1907, in Heritage Park, Calgary. Sudbury, Ontario. June 24, 1974. *(Jim McRae)*

CP 1596 PB series 1580-1599
▶Wood coach #1596 is seen in Orangeville Ontario on May 1, 1960 on the end of a triple-headed steam excursion. In 1907, CPR's Angus Shops in Montreal completed 20 72' six-wheel first-class coaches with smoking room, numbered #780-799. This car, originally #796, was renumbered in January 1912 to #1596. CP wood cars were originally finished in varnished natural wood. In July 1960 CP sold #1596 to Ontario Hydro at Kapuskasing, Ontario. *(Gary R. Zuters)*

CP 782 PB series 600-782
▼In March 1908, Pullman-Standard built this 65' first-class coach as #2428 for the St. John and Boston Line, a joint CPR-B&M-MEC route formed in 1907. In May 1926, the car was allotted to the CPR which renumbered it #782. CP scrapped the wood car in November 1960, one year after this photo in Swift Current, Saskatchewan on October 4, 1959.

(Lou Schmitz)

CP 986 PB series 986-989
▲Built in 1926, steel first-class coach #986 is 75'-6" long. It provides seating for 88 passengers and has ice activated air conditioning. The first CPR steel passenger cars in 1912 were painted a special orange-yellow developed to imitate the color of the varnished wood cars. Sometime after 1917 all passenger cars, both wood and steel, were painted the rich tuscan-red enamel used by the CP subsidiary Soo Line. Windsor, Ontario. September 1959. *(Emery J. Gulash)*

CP 1450 PB series 1425-1469
▶First-class coach #1450 is at St. Gabriel, Quebec on October 4, 1958. It was built in 1923-25, with a length of 75'-6". It provides seating for 74 passengers in its main area and 8 in a smoking room. It is freshly painted with maroon sides and ends and black roof, underframe, steps and diaphrams. *(Gary R. Zuters Collection)*

CP 1322 PB series 1300-1337
▼Built in 1929-31, first-class coach #1322 is 75'-6" long and has seating for 74 in its main section and 8 in a smoking compartment. In 1950 CP owned 989 first-class coaches and 50 second-class coaches. Ottawa, Ontario. 1970. *(Tom Hood)*

CP 1326 PB series 1300-1337
▲Photographed in Windsor Ontario in November 1959, first-class coach #1326 was built 1929-31 and has a length of 75'-6". It seats 74 in its main section and 8 in a smoking compartment.
(Emery J. Gulash)

CP 1350 PB series 1300-1350
▼Originally built as buffet-parlor car #6685, this car was rebuilt to a first-class coach in September 1959, one year before this photo. It was built by CC&F and finished by Angus shops in July 1929. It is 75'6" long and has ice activated air conditioning. In June 1970, CP donated this and 23 similiar cars to the Central Railway of Peru. Toronto, Ontario. September 1960.
(Jim Parker)

CP 1853 PB series 1850-1859
▼First-class coach with smoking room #1853 is seen at Ottawa Union Station in 1957. It was built 1926-30, is 74'-10" long, seats 88 and has ice activated air conditioning. These coaches were used system-wide for commuters, locals and name trains. *(Graham M. Stremes)*

CP 835 PB series 800-839

▲ This commuter coach is in Sudbury Ontario on June 24 1981. Built by CC&F in August 1953, it is 78' long and seats 103. These coaches were used in commuter service into Montreal until 1970 when the bi-level 'gallery' cars were acquired. In 1982 these coaches were sold to STCUM (Montreal Urban Community Transit Corporation) who contracted CP Rail to operate them. It carries the CP RAIL paint scheme. *(Jim McRae)*

CP 922

◀ This is a bi-level 85' coach for commuter service into Montreal's CP Windsor station. Two control cars and seven trailer cars were built by Canadian Vickers Industries Ltd. for CP Rail in June 1969 and started service April 21 1970. The push-pull cars are operated in trains with a locomotive at one end and a control car at the other so that the train is not turned at the terminal. Each control car carries 156 passengers while each coach carries 168. In 1996, these cars are owned and operated by the Montreal Urban Community Transit Corporation. Rigaud, Quebec. June 17, 1979. *(Ronald Plazzotta)*

CP 2103 PB series 2100-2107

▼ This first-class coach had a 36'-10" passenger compartment to seat 36 passengers. At either end of the car are two enclosed lounges with a toilet annex. The ladies' lounge accomodated five passengers while the mens' lounge accomodated ten. The car was built by National Steel Car and finished in Angus Shops in 1936 for new semi-streamlined lightweight trains pulled by high-speed Jubilee class 4-4-4 engines. The coach is 65'-0" long, has two-axle Commonwealth trucks with a 9'-6" wheelbase and ice activated air conditioning. Two of these coaches were on the end of each of the following trains: ROYAL YORK (Toronto-Windsor-Detroit), CHINOOK (Calgary-Edmonton), FRONTENAC and VIGER (Montreal-Quebec City). These were the fastest trains in the country at the time. The window shades are brown. Toronto, Ontario. September 1960. *(Jim Parker)*

CP 2272 PB series 2200-2298

▲This 68-passenger lightweight coach was built in March 1950. It has the CP Rail aluminum paint scheme with the action red stripe and black underframe. The view from the vestibule end was taken in the Sudbury Ontario yard in August 1969. *(Jim McRae)*

CP 2276 PB series 2200-2298

▼This lightweight coach, built in May 1950, carries maroon sides and ends, black roof and underframe. It is in the Toronto coach yard in 1968. On September 29, 1978, CP Rail transferred its passenger car fleet and services to the new Via Rail Canada. *(Coo/West Collection)*

CP 2296 PB series 2200-2298

▼Another of the lightweight coaches, built in September 1950, carries the standard maroon sides and ends, black roof and underframe. This view of the non-vestibule end was taken beside the Sudbury Ontario station in August 1969. In 1973 BC Rail acquired this car and named it *Sundance*. *(Jim McRae)*

Combines

CP 3358 CO series 3350-3365
▲This standard 65' wood baggage-passenger combine was photographed at Haycroft Ontario in October 1959. It was built in Angus shops in April 1909 as #1579 and renumbered in December 1910 to 3279. In April 1933 it was renumbered 3358 and ultimately scrapped at Angus Shops in January 1960, three months after this photo. These combines were commonly used in branch line and mixed-train service. *(Emery J. Gulash)*

CP 3262 CA series 3260-3299
▼Seen in Toronto in September 1960, this 65' wood baggage-smoker combine was built in September 1912 in CP's Angus shops. It is one of 40 similar combines. Although in need of paint, it clearly shows the standard paint scheme of maroon sides and black baggage-end, roof and underframe. The car was scrapped at Angus shops in September 1961. In 1950 CP owned 57 combination cars. *(Jim Parker)*

CP *Glen Major* PS *Glen* series
▲This 10-compartment sleeping car, one of nine *Glen* cars built in 1926 by CC&F, is 75'-0" long and accommodates 40 passengers. Ice activated air conditioning was installed in 1937. It was converted to company service flat car #418125 in December 1961. It is named for a town on the Trenton Division, Ontario. Toronto, Ontario. September 1960.
(Jim Parker)

CP *Glennariff* PS *Glen* series
▼This 10-compartment sleeping car, one of five *Glen* cars built in 1927 by CC&F, is 75'-0" long and accommodates 40. It was remodelled and air-conditioned in 1945 and was in the 1951 Royal Train of Princess Elizabeth and Prince Phillip. It is shown awaiting scrapping in Ogden Shops in Calgary in January 1970. In 1950 CP owned 454 sleeping cars. *(John Riddell)*

CP *Steelton* PS 'S' series
▲ *Steelton* is one of 65 'S' series sleepers built in 1930-31 by CC&F and completed at CP's Angus shops. It has 12 sections and 1 drawing room, is air-conditioned and is shown in Vancouver B.C. in May 1968. The 'S' sleepers were named for towns on the CP. Steelton is on the Sudbury Division, Ontario. *(Stan Styles, John Riddell Collection)*

CP *Richford* PS 'R' series
◄ One of the 29 'R' series sleepers is shown in Sudbury Ontario. It has 8 sections, 1 drawing room and two compartments and is named for a town in Vermont on the Farnham Division. These tuscan red heavyweight sleeping cars last served on the ATLANTIC LIMITED between Montreal and Saint John, New Brunswick in 1969. *Richford* was scrapped in June 1975. CP owned and operated its own sleeping cars as opposed to contracting with the Pullman Company as was common for U.S. railroads. One exception was the Montreal-Chicago route on which CP and Pullman sleeping cars shared the traffic. *(Dale Wilson)*

CP *Pine Grove* PS *Grove* series
▼ This view of the corridor-side of lightweight sleeping car *Pine Grove* was taken in Toronto in September 1968. It has aluminum paint with maroon stripes and gold lettering for visual compatibility with the newer stainless-steel cars. *(Bill Coo/West Collection)*

CP *Walnut Grove* PS Grove series
▲This is one of 19 lightweight roomette sleeping cars containing 10 roomettes and 5 double-bedrooms. It accommodates ten in its bedrooms and ten in its roomettes. It has mechanical air conditioning and was built in July 1950 by National Steel Car Co. and finished by Angus shops. These cars were named for groves of tree species. This view shows the bedroom-side of the car in Toronto, Ontario. April 1956. *(Stan Styles, John Riddell Collection)*

CP *Palm Grove* PS Grove series
▼This view of the corridor-side of the non-vestibule end shows the paint scheme on a roomette sleeper in Sudbury Ontario in 1966. The green window shades are drawn to keep the sun from heating the car. This car was also sold in March 1976 to the National Railways of Mexico.
(Dale Wilson)

CP 6400 DC series 6400-6401

▲Restaurant Car #6400 was built in March 1933 from Cafe-Parlor car #68. The latter had been built in Angus Shops in February 1907 for the Montreal and Boston Air Line, a joint CPR - Boston and Maine operation. #6400 is 72'0" long and was scrapped in July 1954. CP had a total of four different Restaurant Cars. September 1, 1951. *(W.J. McChesney)*

CP *Alnwick* DA 'A'-series

▼This is one of eight 'A' series dining cars built in 1931 by National Steel Car and completed at Angus shops. The view shows the kitchen side. It seats 36 for dining and had ice-activated air conditioning installed in 1936. The cooking fuel is coal. It is shown in Vancouver B.C. in July 1968. In 1950 CP owned 97 dining cars. *(Stan Styles, John Riddell Collection)*

Observation Cars

CP *Cape Beale* PO *Cape* series
▲This is one of 15 78' Solarium-Lounge cars built in 1929, named for rivers. The car shells were built by National Steel Car and the interiors were finished at Angus Shops. It is a buffet-compartment-solarium observation-sleeper having 1 compartment, 4 double-bedrooms, 8 chairs and 17 seats. Originally *River Tyne*, in 1941 this car was rebuilt with ice activated air-conditioning and renamed *Cape Tyne*. In 1946 it was again renamed *Cape Beale*. In the background are boxcars fitted with icicle breakers. Ogden Shops, Calgary. January 1970. *(John Riddell)*

CP *Cape Bauld* PO *Cape* series
▼Built in 1929 as *River Moira*, this car was rebuilt in 1941 as *Cape Moira* and renamed in 1946 *Cape Bauld*. They were used in transcontinental service on THE TRANS-CANADA LIMITED, THE DOMINION, THE MOUNTAINEER and THE KETTLE VALLEY EXPRESS. Subsidiary Soo Line owned four identical cars. Canadian Pacific's Royal York hotel is in the background. Toronto, Ontario. May 1967. *(Jim Parker)*

15

CP *Seaview* PS *View* series

▲This is one of four 5 double-bedroom buffet-lounge observation cars built by the Budd Company in 1949 for the New York Central which named it #10560, *Babbling Brook*. CP purchased four such NYC cars in January 1959 - CP named the others *Eastview*, *Mountain View* and *Riverview*. These cars were commonly used on the tail end of Toronto-Ottawa overnight trains. CP sold *Seaview* in August 1969 to the Quebec Cartier Mining Company. Toronto, Ontario. June 1964. *(Jim Parker)*

CP 7908 PO series 7900-7915

▼CP operated several types of wood mountain-observation cars. Sixteen open observation cars for use in the mountains were built from 1922 to 1928. Five were built without roofs but had roofs added within two years. #7908 is shown on the end of an east-bound train at the station at Banff, Alberta in July 1952. It was built in May 1922 from Colonist car #146 which had been built by Crossen Car Works in 1884. It is one of seven cars with 50'0" length over sills and 64 seating capacity. The center seating section is enclosed while both ends are open. Nine similar cars were 56'0" over end sills. #7908 was scrapped at Ogden Shops in November 1952. *(W.J. McChesney)*

CP 598 PO series 597-599

▼CP built this steel mountain-observation car from coach #1422 in June 1956. Like its two companions, it seats 96 passengers and was commonly used between Calgary and Vancouver on the end of THE MOUNTAINEER and THE DOMINION. It was sold to the West Coast Railway Association in May 1965 and is preserved in West Coast Railway Museum, Squamish, B.C. It is shown at Vancouver, British Columbia in June 1967. *(Jim Parker)*

The Canadian Cars

CP 3017 CSB series 3008-3017
▲This is one of 18 baggage-dormitory cars built by the Budd Company in January 1955 for THE CANADIAN. It contains sleeping accomodation for 18 crew members as well as a 47' baggage compartment. Two crews worked THE CANADIAN - one between Montreal/Toronto and Winnipeg and the other between Winnipeg and Vancouver. This car was scrapped after being damaged in a wreck near Hinton, Alberta in February 1986 while in Via service. This view shows the corridor-side of the car in Toronto, Ontario in May 1967. *(Jim Parker)*

CP 110 PB series 100-129
▲This is one of 30 first-class coaches built in May 1955 by the Budd Company. It seats 36 plus 24 in smoking room. CP ordered 173 fluted-side cars for THE CANADIAN from the Budd Company in June 1953 - the largest single order ever received by Budd - a total value of $40 million ($400 million in 1996 dollars).Toronto, Ontario. September 1964. *(Jim Parker)*

CP 111 PB series 100-129
▼This is one of 30 first-class coaches built in May 1955 by the Budd Company. It seats 36 plus 24 in smoking compartment. Canoe, British Columbia. June 1967. *(Jim Parker)*

CP 514 DB *Skyline* series 500-517
▲One of 18 first-class dome-coach-buffet cars built in February 1955. It is 79' long, CP Rail paint. CP implemented a crash program from February to June 1969 to repaint the stainless steel cars to the new CP Rail scheme. The work was done in the Glen Yard roundhouse in Montreal. This view shows the kitchen-side of the diner in Calgary, Alberta on September 29, 1976.*(Ronald Plazzotta)*

CP 515 DB *Skyline* series 500-517
▼This is another of the 18 first-class dome-coach-buffet built in January 1955. 79' long, It seats 49 in its coach section and 24 in its dome section. This shot showing the original CP paint scheme was taken at Revelstoke, British Columbia in June 1967. *(Jim Parker)*

CP *Chateau Radisson* PS *Chateau* series
▼This is one of 29 sleeping cars containing four sections, eight duplex roomettes, one drawing room and three double-bedrooms. The *Chateau* sleepers carried names of French Canadians prominent in Canadian history. The upper berth duplex roomettes of *Chateau* sleepers required two higher windows on each side of the car. Budd built the car in September 1954. It shows the original CANADIAN paint scheme with the cast beaver shields by the doors and two tuscan red stripes with gold lettering. This view shows the corridor-side of the car in John Street yard, Toronto, Ontario. October 1967. *(Bill Coo, Coo/West Collection)*

CP *Carlton Manor* PS *Manor* series

▲This is one of 42 sleeping cars containing four sections, four roomettes, one compartment and five double-bedrooms. The *Manor* sleepers carried names of persons of British ancestory prominent in Canadian history. Long tuscan red panels carry CANADIAN PACIFIC in gold lettering above the windows. A thin tuscan stripe is on the belt rail moulding below the windows. 1946-style cast beaver shields were mounted beside the vestibule doors. It was built by Budd in December 1954. This view shows the corridor-side of the car in Toronto Ontario. May 1967. *(Jim Parker)*

CP *Blair Manor* PS *Manor* series

▲While these sleeping cars were built for THE CANADIAN, during off-peak season many were used regularly on the transcontinental DOMINION and shorter routes in Ontario and Quebec. On October 29, 1978, CP Rail sold its 168 remaining stainless steel cars to Via Rail Canada which subsequently rebuilt 150 of the cars for continued transcontinental service. Toronto, Ontario. July 1973. *(Jim Parker)*

CP *Champlain* DA series 16501-16518

▼*Champlain* is one of 18 dining cars named for a dining room, public room or lounge of a Canadian Pacific-owned hotel. It included seating for 48 in addition to its kitchen. Each named dining car, featuring a mural of its namesake hotel, also had a number. This one, #16506, was built by Budd in February 1955. The kitchen-side of the car is shown in Sudbury, Ontario in September 1976. *(Jim Parker)*

CP *Assiniboine Park* PO *Park* series
▲*Assiniboine Park* is one of 18 observation cars named for national or provincial parks. It has one drawing-room, three double-bedrooms, a buffet-lounge located under a 24-seat dome, and a round-end observation end. It is named for Assiniboine Provincial Park in British Columbia near Banff. Budd built the car in October 1954. Revelstoke, British Columbia. June 1967. *(Jim Parker)*

CP *Sibley Park* PO *Park* series
▼Each of the 18 *Park* observation cars featured paintings depicting scenes and maps of their namesake provincial or national park. Sibley Provincial Park is near Thunder Bay, Ontario on Lake Superior. Car names, at the center of the car, are in tuscan red with gold outline. This car was built by Budd in September 1954. Operating daily between Montreal/Toronto and Vancouver, these dome cars provided the longest dome car journey in the world. Canoe, British Columbia. June 1967. *(Jim Parker)*

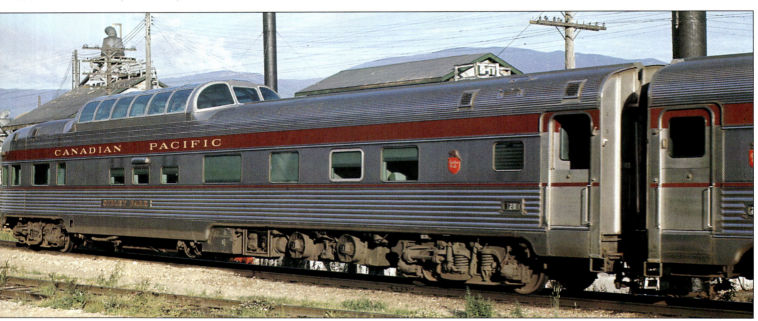

CP *Kokanee Park* PO *Park* series
▼In 1968 CP Rail painted the cars with Action Red striping and CP Rail multi-mark and lettering, and removed the cast beaver shields. The CP Rail tail-end sign is displayed on the end. Kokanee Provincial Park is in southern British Columbia near Nelson. Each *Park* car featured a mural by a prominent Canadian artist in its cocktail lounge. This car had a mural painting by A.Y. Jackson depicting Kokanee Park. Thunder Bay, Ontario. September 21, 1976. *(Ronald Plazzotta)*

 Head-End Cars

CP 4479 BE series 4434-4479
▲This baggage and express car was built in January 1928 by National Steel Car as Through-Baggage #4943 for express shipments of highly-perishable silk from Vancouver to New York City. It has an interior length of 44'-0" and a 6'0" wide door. In July 1949 it was converted to Baggage and Express car #4479 which is shown at Chatham, Ontario in August 1962. CP had two series of steel 'silk cars' which were used in high-speed silk trains until the thirties.

(Emery J. Gulash)

CP 4167 BE series 4141-4174
▼This standard 60' baggage and express car was built in October 1913 by CC&F. A steel underframe was applied in February 1919. It has gas lighting. It is shown at Vancouver on November 26, 1960 freshly painted in standard paint scheme of tuscan sides, black roof, ends, underframe and door sills. It was scrapped at Ogden shops in 1961. *(Doug Cummings, Lou Schmitz Collection)*

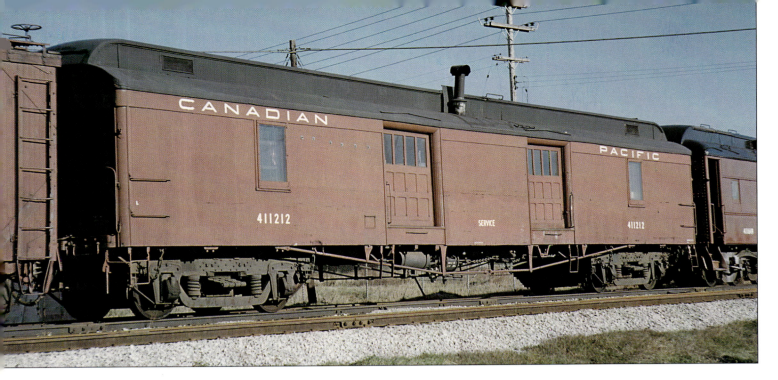

CP 411212 BE ex-series 1759-1999

▲This standard wood baggage-express car is in company service with a service number and stencilling in white block letters. It was built as #1858 in 1909 by Angus shops. It was renumbered #3967 and then converted to service in May 1957 as #411212. CP owned approximately 300 such cars. Windsor, Ontario. November 1959. *(Emery J. Gulash)*

CP 4480 BE series 4480-4483

◄#4480 is a steel arch-roof baggage & express built in October 1930 by National Steel Car as #4470. The inside length is 79'-11". In February 1949 it was renumered #4480. Windsor, Ontario. September 1959.
(Emery J. Gulash)

CP 4554 BH series 4554-4559

▼This steel horse-express car was built in May 1929 as #4480. It was renumbered #4422 in November 1943 and again renumbered #4554 in April 1958. It has an inside length of 79'-11" and was built by CC&F and Angus shops. CP owned 57 horse-express cars of various types over the years. Calgary, Alberta. October 3, 1959.

(Lou Schmitz)

CP 4722 BE series 4700-4789
▲One of 89 baggage and express cars built by CC&F between October 1952 and October 1953. It has an inside length of 80'4". The smooth side car is painted to match the stainless steel cars. Toronto, Ontario. May 1967. *(Jim Parker)*

CP 3846 BE formerly series 3830-3865
▼#3846 is a standard wood 60' baggage mail and express car containing a 30' baggage section and a 30' mail section. It was built 1909 at Angus shops as #2098. In December 1910 it was renumbered #3452. A steel underframe was applied in August 1926. In April 1956 it was renumbered #3846 and in August 1961 scrapped at Ogden shops. In January 1956 CP had 48 similiar cars in service. #3846 served many years in southern B.C and is shown at Swift Current, Saskatchewan on October 4, 1959. *(Lou Schmitz)*

CP 4215 BE series 4200-4256
▼This steel baggage and express car was built in June 1947 by Canadian Car & Foundry. It has a length over end-frames of 81'-0" and door openings of 10'-1" and 6'-1". It is shown in Calgary in April 1974. In 1950 CP owned 620 baggage, express and postal cars. *(John Riddell)*

CP 2503 BH ex-series 4560-4565
▲This is one of six steel Horse Express cars built in 1949 as series 4560-4565. It has been renumbered to #2503. It is 81'-0" over end sills and has large end doors on one end. It is shown at the Calgary stock yards in April 1974. *(John Riddell)*

CP 29106 XM series 29019-29115
◀This 40' box-express car is equipped for passenger train service with steam and signal lines and U-C air brakes. It was built in July 1937 and carries the standard passenger color scheme of tuscan sides, black ends, roof and ladders. Weston Shops, Winnipeg. August 1983. *(F. Headon)*

CP 4907 BX
▼This 40' box-express car, built in August 1937, is equipped for passenger train service. This car, formerly numbered in series 29019-29115, is painted aluminum with maroon lettering to match the stainless steel cars of THE CANADIAN. It is at the Calgary station in July 1975.
(Tom Hood)

CP 5836 BS series 5830-5854
▲CP took delivery of 105 8-hatch express reefers for passenger train service. They were built between 1950 and 1954 by National Steel Car Co. and were assigned four number series. This car, built March 1953, has a steel mesh roof walk, an Ajax brake wheel and National Steel Car type ends. The liquidometer temperature indicator is below the 'M' stencil. The paint and lettering scheme is as-delivered for passenger service. It has maroon sides, black ends, roof and underframe. The lines above 'CP' and below the car number were not applied in later lettering. The car is at Haycroft Ontario, 21 miles east of Windsor, in October 1959. *(Emery J. Gulash)*

CP 5618 BR series 5600-5699
▼One of 100 steel-underframe express refrigerator cars is shown in Toronto circa 1956. These cars, built in 1922 by the Canadian Car and Foundry, have an outside length of 45'-10", 5'-wide doors, Murphy metal roof, eight brine tanks - four per end, and fish-belly centre sills. The 7' wheel-base trucks have 36" wheels. The capacity is 60,000 lbs. The car carries standard CPR passenger colors of maroon sides, black ends, sidesills, ladders, roof and underframe and gold lettering. *(Gary R. Zuters Collection)*

Official Cars

CP 1
▲Business Car #1 was built circa 1870 by Crossen Car Co. of Cobourg, Ontario as St. Lawrence & Ottawa Railway's Business Car #9. On October 5, 1882 CP purchased the car from the St.L&O and renumbered it #77, then #78, then #14 and finally in 1907, #1. This is one of two CP cars that carried the number '1' and coincidentally is the oldest existing CP business car. It is 45'10" long and has Pintsch gas lighting and a baker heater. The exterior is whitewood while the interior is walnut and ash. The car is preserved in the Canadian Railway Museum at Delson, Quebec. Ottawa, Ontario, 1974. *(Tom Hood)*

CP 3
▼Business Car #3 was in Sudbury, Ontario when photographed in May 1968. The 60'8" car was built by CP in July 1929 as *Manitoba* - the fourth business car to carry that name. In 1961 it was assigned #3 for a Division Superintendent. *(Jim McRae)*

CP 4

▶Wood Business Car #4, 67'1" long, was completed July 28, 1886 by the Crossen Car Co. in Cobourg, Ontario as sleeper *Australia*. It was subsequently named *St. Andrews*, *Saskatchewan*, *Champlain* and finally numbered #4 in January 1934. It was scrapped in 1959. CP has owned 123 'official' cars over the years, assigning them 50 different names and 77 numbers which were used 242 times. The number '13' has never been assigned. In 1955, 64 official cars were in use. Twenty-six carried names and were assigned to officers of General Superintendent's rank and above. Twenty-six others were numbered 1 through 39 and assigned to Division Superintendents. Twelve other numbered cars were special cars such as instruction, dynamometer, pay and vision test cars. Smiths Falls, Ontario. May 1956. *(Jim Parker)*

CP 7

▲This business car was completed in December 1928 as *Algoma* - the second car to carry that name. It was renumbered to #7 on August 13, 1969 and was assigned to the Sudbury Division superintendent when photographed in Sudbury in December 1970. It is 60'8" long and contains a bedroom, secretary's room, observation room, dining room and steward's room. It has no air conditioning. This car is preserved near Uxbridge, Ontario. *(Jim McRae)*

CP 10

▼This business car was built in November 1928 as *Ontario* - the fourth car to carry that name. It was renumbered #10 on June 8, 1962. It was assigned to the Smiths Falls Division superintendent when photographed in Smiths Falls in July 1969. It is 73' long and has no air conditioning. *(Tom Hood)*

CP 12
◀ This Business Car was built in April 1930 as business car *Saskatchewan* - the fourth car to carry that name. It was renumbered #12 on June 20, 1962. It is 60'-8" long. It was assigned to the Revelstoke Division superintendent when photographed in Vancouver, B.C. on September 22, 1980. It is non air conditioned.

(David Stremes)

CP 23
▼ Business Car #23 was built on June 30, 1896 for Quebec Central Railway. In 1912 CP assigned it to the QCR with name *Megantic*. On August 23 1935 CP renamed it *Beauce*. It was renumbered #23 on September 26 1939. It is 62'-2" long. Smiths Falls, Ontario. July 1965. *(Jim Parker)*

CP 30
▼ Business Car #30 was built 1927 by National Steel Car as *Fort Simpson*, one of five *Fort* class steel observation sleepers. It contained 6 sections, 2 compartments, buffet and 12-seat lounge. From 12/57 to 07/60 this car served as the last pay car on the CP making a weekly run between Megantic, Quebec and Mattawamkeag, Maine to pay remote employees on the International of Maine Division. In July 1960 it was converted to an official car by removing several sections to provide a seperate dining room. In July 1962 it was renumbered to #30 and in 1974 was sold to J. Bosworth Ltd. Smiths Falls, Ontario. February 1971. *(Tom Hood)*

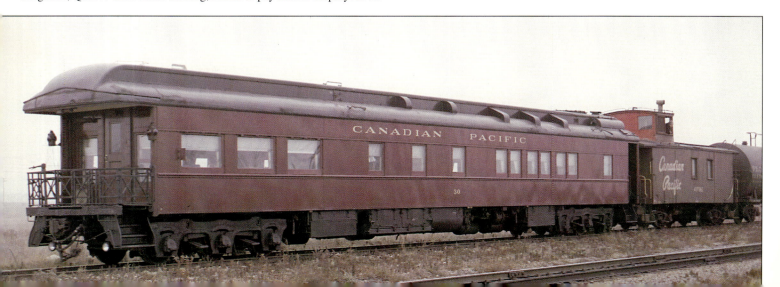

CP 46
▲Business car #46 is at the station in Fredericton, New Brunswick on October 19, 1965. It was one of 38 cars built in 1929-31 by National Steel Car as First-Class Coaches with smoking room. #1308 was 75'6" long and seated 74 plus 8 in the smoking room. In 1963, it was renumbered #46. *(James L. O'Donnell)*

CP 60
▼Official car #60 is a mechanical instruction car pictured at Smiths Falls, Ontario in May 1978. It was built June 6, 1941 from wood observation car *Mount Hurd* that had been built in 1909 as sleeper-observation *Glenside*. It is steel-sheathed and 73'-3" long. This car is preserved at Tottenham, Ontario by the South Simcoe Railway Heritage Corp. *(Tom Hood)*

CP 62
▼This dynamometer car was built in 1928 by Angus Shops to replace two older wood dynamometer cars, #63 and #64. It is equipped with apparatus for measuring and recording drawbar pull, horsepower, brakepipe pressure and other data connected with locomotive performance and train haul conditions. It has a capacity of 500,000 lb. of drawbar pull. It has a steel superstructure, 60' long over frame, canvas-covered wood roof, hot water heating, The 16'-long taller end contains a recording room with chronograph while the lower part includes bedroom, dining room, kitchen, steward's room and lavatory. It carries CP Rail yellow lettering with a yellow and black multimark although it is owned by the National Research Council of Canada. CP Rail presented the car to the NRC in 1975. This view shows the car's corridor-side at Sudbury, Ontario on August 18, 1983. *(Jim McRae)*

CP 76

▲This car was present at the driving of the last spike of the CPR in 1885. It is shown in Heritage Park, Calgary, Alberta, May 1974, restored to its appearance in 1885. The body is yellow-ochre with lettering in gold leaf outlined in black. The 48' car was built in 1882 by Harlan & Hollingsworth for CPR contractors Langdon, Shepard & Company. CP subsequently numbered it #71, #76, *Rosemere*, *New Brunswick*, and again *Rosemere*. CP sold it in 1929 to the Edmonton Dunvegan & British Columbia Railway, which named it *Dunvegan*. Later it became official car #3 of the Northern Alberta Railway. *(John Riddell)*

CP 22

◀This is one of 22 35' business cars for Division Superintendents across the system. It was built from a caboose on April 15, 1903 and numbered #36. It was renumbered #22 on December 3 1906. Division business cars were numbered 1 through 39. The car carries white service lettering. It provides accomodation for the official and an attendent. This car spent its career in British Columbia and was scrapped in November 1961 at Nelson, B.C. Vancouver B.C. December 9, 1961. *(Doug Cummings, Lou Schmitz Collection)*

CP *Mount Stephen*

◀This Business Car was built by CP on December 23, 1926. Ice activated air conditioning was installed at Angus Shops in October 1937. It is steam heated and uses coal as cooking fuel. In 1980 it was assigned to the Public Relations Department for system-wide use. The car is named for a prominent mountain beside the line in the Rockies. The car length is 74'-6". It is in Glen Yard, Montreal on August 19, 1977. *(J. Bryce Lee, Coo/West Collection)*

CP *Van Horne*
▲This Business Car was built by CP on May 14, 1927. Air conditioned in 1937. In 1980 this car was assigned to the Vice-President Pacific Region. The car is named for William Van Horne, the man responsible for constructing the line to the Pacific in 1885 and later company President. The car length is 74'6". Calgary, Alberta. July 1968. *(John Riddell)*

CP *Assiniboine*
▲This is the third CP business car to carry the name *Assiniboine*. Many names were applied multiple times. The most frequently used name, *British Columbia*, was carried seven times by six different business cars. This Business Car was built by CP on December 12, 1929. The 77' car was air-conditioned in May 1947. It is named for a prominent Indian tribe of the Prairies. In 1980 *Assiniboine* was assigned to the company President. Toronto, Ontario. July 18, 1994. *(Gary R. Zuters)*

CP *Lacombe*
▼Business car *Lacombe* was photographed in Smiths Falls, Ontario on March 24, 1985. It was built April 26 1943 from compartment sleeper *Glen Roy* which had been built August 1921. It is named for Father Lacombe, an Oblate priest who in 1883 successfully negotiated the right-of-way through a Blackfoot indian reserve on behalf of the CPR with Chief Crowfoot. In 1980 this 74'6" car was assigned to the General Manager, Operation and Maintenance, Eastern Region. *(David. P. Stremes)*

Boxcars

36' BOX CARS

CP 401881 XM series 401582-401999
▲This truss-rod wood boxcar has arch-bar trucks and wood ends. It was rebuilt in June 1928 with reinforced ends and is in company service as a block car. Ottawa West, Ontario 1958. *(Graham Stremes)*

CP 30272 XM series 30203-30351
▼Lime was shipped in boxcars with roof hatches such as #30272 seen at Ottawa West in 1954. The wood car was built in 1918 and rebuilt in July 1928 to a Lime car with roof hatches, reversed Murphy steel ends and a steel center sill. The black panel requests RETURN EMPTY TO FARM POINT QUE VIA OTTAWA. Capacity is 2460 cu. ft. *(Graham Stremes)*

CP 30203 XM series 30203-30351
▲Another wood boxcar for lime has roof hatches, a steel fish-belly underframe, reversed Murphy steel ends and arch-bar trucks. It was built in February 1918. The black panel indicates RETURN EMPTY TO FARM POINT QUE VIA OTTAWA. BRUCITE ONLY. On the right is another CP Lime Car #30344 built from a Fowler patent box car. Capacity is 2460 cu. ft. Ottawa West, 1954. *(Graham Stremes)*

CP 403115 XM
Ex-series 195903-197999
▲This turn-of-the-century wood car with truss rods and arch-bar trucks is still in company service on CP's subsidiary Dominion Atlantic Railway in Windsor, Nova Scotia, September 12, 1964. The car has been rebuilt with steel center sill and dreadnaught ends. *(James O'Donnell)*

CP 220811 XM
series 220000-220999
▶Built in 1923, this 36' boxcar has reversed Murphy steel ends and a steel fish-belly underframe. The white placard says THIS CAR NOT TO BE LOADED FOR DESTINATION IN UNITED STATES. It has been retired with a coupler missing in Agincourt Yard, Toronto in August 1979. Capacity is 2639 cu. ft. *(John Riddell)*

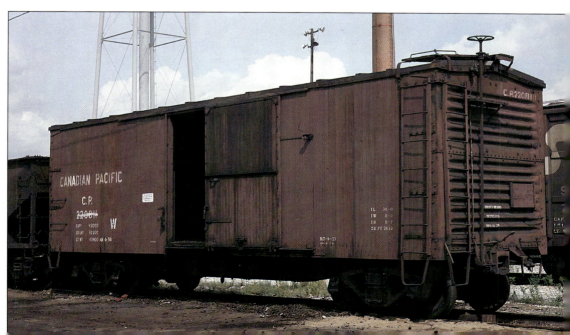

CP 422812 XM Ex-series 220000-220999
◀ This 36' material service car, built as #220342 in 1928, has a steel fish-belly underframe, reversed Murphy steel ends, steel roof and arch-bar trucks. Cranbrook, British Columbia. September 28, 1974. *(John Riddell)*

CP 191220 XM series 170069-193121
▼ From 1896 to 1913 CP experienced unprecedented growth of its traffic, especially in Western Canada. To handle this great increase, from 1909 to 1915 CP purchased more than 33,000 36' single-sheathed steel-frame boxcars of the Fowler-patent - the largest fleet of single-sheathed boxcars owned by any railroad. These boxcars served for many years with 65 still in revenue service in 1965. #191220 retains its revenue number in a work train at Canmore Alberta on a sunny July morning in 1979. In the background is the front range of the Rocky Mountains. *(John Riddell)*

CP 422575 XM series 170069-193121
◀ These 36' single-sheathed boxcars were designed by CP's design group under W.E. Fowler, CP's Master Car Builder at the time. Fowler later obtained a Canadian patent on a feature of the design. The cars were built by 10 different builders in Canada and the U.S. In 1945, 27,840 of these durable 36' boxcars still constituted 33% of the CP boxcar fleet. #422575 carries a company service number in a work train. It appears that a barrel of oil had been spilled in the car at some time. Capacity is 2450 cu. ft. Canmore, Alberta. July 1979.

(John Riddell)

40' COMPOSITE BOXCARS

CP 235238 XM series 234000-238536
▲During World War I, the United States Railroad Administration developed a design for a single-sheathed boxcar. The CP used the basic USRA-design except for incorporating Murphy 7-8 corrugated ends and Burnett grain hopper doors in the floor beneath each door. In 1920-21, CP bought 3,500 of these steel-frame cars numbered 230000-233499 - 2,000 from Canadian Car and Foundry, 1,000 from National Steel Car and 500 from Eastern Car. During the mid 1930's CP renumbered and rebuilt the cars removing the hopper doors, installing AB brakes, power hand-brakes and cast side-frame trucks. This car was built in March 1921 and has a capacity of 3098 cu. ft. July 1971. *(Tom Hood)*

CP 236636 XM series 234000-238536
▼In July 1975, 40' single-sheathed box-car #236636 was spotted beside the roundhouse at Esquimalt, B.C. Built in 1921, it had a Camel 6' door, Murphy metal roof, AB brakes and an inside length of 40'6". In July 1960, 2,477 of these boxcars were still in service but by January 1983 only five were left. *(Tom Hood)*

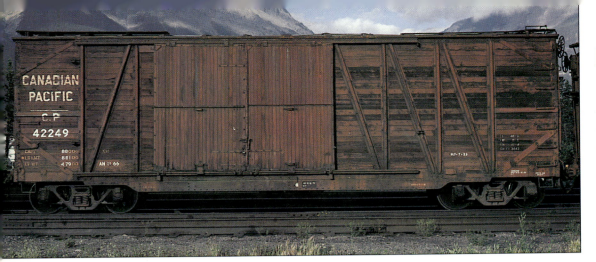

DOUBLE-DOOR BOXCARS

CP 42249 XM
series 42000-42299
◀ This steel-frame car with staggered doors over a 10' opening was built in July 1923. It has an inside height of 10'0" and capacity of 3442 cu. ft. and was originally in series 297000-298099. Canmore, Alberta. July 1979. *(John Riddell)*

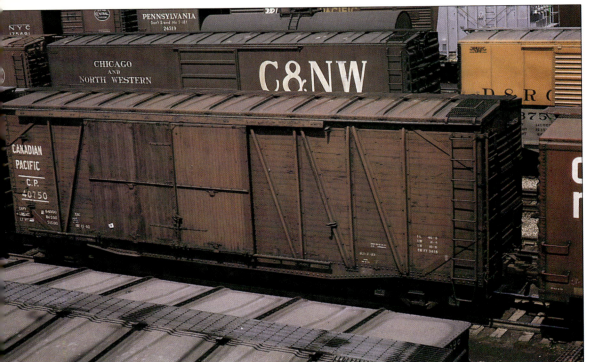

CP 40750 XM
series 40580-40753
◀ In May 1964 #40750 was in a yard in Columbus, Ohio. It has staggered doors over a 10' opening and a steel roof with steel running boards. Its 10'6" inside height provides a 3615 cu. ft. capacity. It was built in July 1923. *(Paul C. Winters)*

CP 403164 XM
Ex-series 296000-296259
▼ This wood-body steel fishbelly underframe automobile-furniture boxcar is seen in Smiths Falls, Ontario in June 1961. It has an inside length of 40'-6" and a 10' door-opening with one and a half doors. The car was built between 1909-12, rebuilt in 1917 and is shown with a service number. CP applies 400000 series numbers to company service equipment. Capacity is 3895 cu. ft. *(Graham Stremes)*

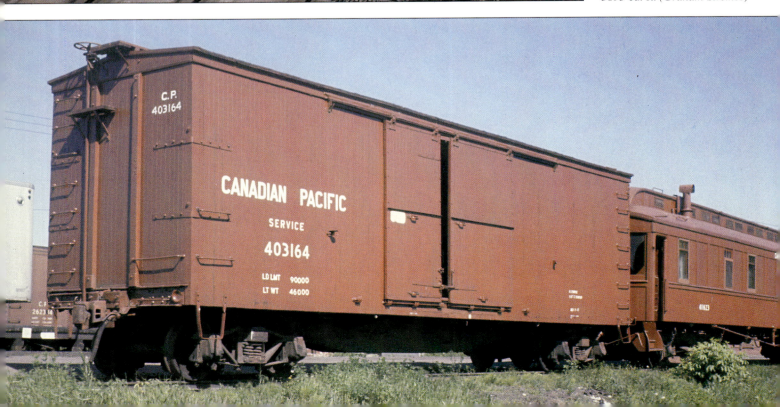

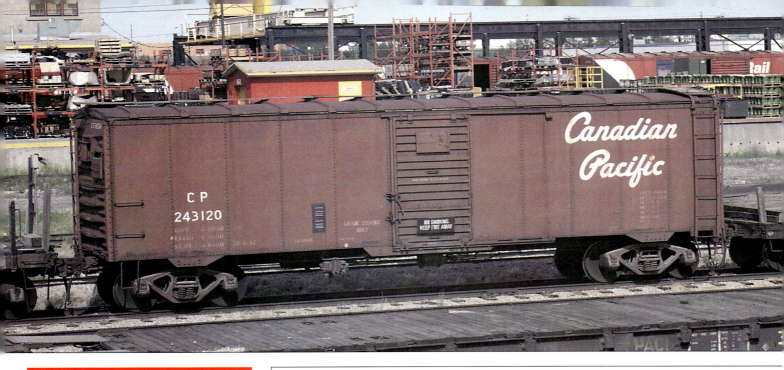

MINIBOX

CP 243120 XM series 240000-247499
▲In 1929, CP purchased 7,500 of these boxcars - its first large orders of steel freight cars - from National Steel Car, Canadian Car & Foundry and Eastern Car. (There were previously several small orders of other steel cars.) It has an 8'-7" interior height, 40'-6" inside length, Murphy radial all-steel flexible roof, Youngstown 5' door and a capacity of 3005 cu. ft. It carried script lettering when photographed at Ogden Shops, Calgary on July 16, 1988. This car is in company service but retains its original revenue number. To the left of the door is stencilled GRAIN SERVICE ONLY. In 1950, CP carried 5.1 million tons of grain, much of it in boxcars like this.
(John Riddell)

CP 404393 XM Ex-series 240000-247499
▶These low 8'-7" interior height boxcars are sometimes referred to as 'mini boxcars' by modelers. This one, in company service, carried stepped gothic lettering when photographed at Agincourt Yard, Toronto on February 20, 1983. These were very common. Of the 7,500 built in 1929, 7,227 were still in revenue service in July 1960. *(John Riddell)*

CP 404394 XM Ex-series 240000-247499
▶This car, in a service number, is one of 1,000 of the series that had an end-door in its A-end for lumber loading. It has a capacity of 3005 cu. ft. and retains its running boards. These cars had the one-line CANADIAN PACIFIC on the left of the door from 1929 until 1947 when the "Spans-the-World" logo was introduced, followed in 1951 by the stepped gothic lettering and finally the script lettering as on this car. It is likely that none of these cars received the CP Rail action red paint. The faded original CANADIAN PACIFIC lettering can be seen on the left side. Agincourt Yard, Toronto. July 22, 1988. *(Gary R. Zuters)*

STANDARD

CP 250202 XM series 249500-250499
▲CP 250202 is one of 1,000 cars built in October 1944 by Canadian Car and Foundry. It has 5/5 dreadnaught ends, raised-panel roof, Ajax handbrake, 6' Youngstown doors, inside height 10'-0" and a capacity of 3715 cu. ft. The car, delivered in the single-line lettering, was painted with script lettering at Angus shops in December 1963. Toronto, Ontario. July 1965. *(Jim Parker)*

CP 250582 XM series 250500-251249
◀ This is one of 750 cars built by Canadian Car and Foundry in 1945. It has an interior height of 10'0", 5/5 dreadnaught ends, raised-panel roof, Ajax handbrake, Youngstown 6' door and a capacity of 3715 cu. ft. The stencil to left of door reads TO BE USED EXCLUSIVELY FOR NEWSPRINT PAPER FLOUR AND SUGAR OR HIGH CLASS MERCHANDISE. Newsprint has long been an important commodity for CP. In 1950 CP carried 1.5 million tons of it. Toronto, Ontario. May 1963. *(Jim Parker)*

CP 252279 XM series 252250-253999
◀ This is one of 1,750 50-ton boxcars built in 1947-48 by Canadian Car and Foundry. It has interior height of 10'6", Youngstown 6' door, improved Dreadnaught ends, raised-panel roof, Ajax handbrake and a capacity of 3900 cu. ft. The car was painted at Ogden Shops in December 1968. Boxcars were built with 6' doors until 1955 after which all new cars had 8' doors. This series of boxcars were the first cars delivered in the Spans-the-World lettering. Smiths Falls, Ontario. July 1969.

(Tom Hood)

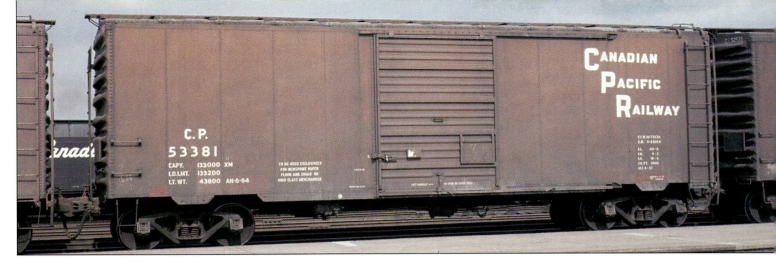

CP 53381 XM series 53200-54199
▲CP 53381 is in Smiths Falls, Ontario in 1966. This is one of 1,000 all-welded boxcars built by Canadian Car and Foundry in 1957. It has improved dreadnaught ends, diagonal-panel roof, Ajax handbrake, and a Superior 5-panel ribbed 8' door. The inside height is 10'6" and capacity is 3900 cu. ft. These cars were delivered in the stepped gothic lettering. *(Graham Stremes)*

CP 54754 XM series 54200-55199
▼In 1957 National Steel Car built this car as one of 1,000 boxcars. It has NSC-type-3 ends, Pullman-Standard single-rib panel roof, Canadian Cardwell handbrake, Youngstown 8' door, 10'6" inside height and a capacity of 3900 cu. ft. Toronto, Ontario. July 1965. *(Jim Parker)*

CP 57005 XM series 56825-57024
▼The red shield indicates this car is for NEWSPRINT SERVICE ONLY. It is one of 200 cars built in 1959 by National Steel Car with NSC type-3 ends, Pullman-Standard type roof, Universal handbrake and Youngstown 8' door. It has a capacity of 3900 cu. ft. The stepped gothic CANADIAN PACIFIC RAILWAY lettering was introduced in 1950. The top of the 'C' is 14 3/4" down from the top of the car side. The right edge of the 'Y' is 2'-6 1/2" from the end rivet row. Toronto, Ontario. July 1965. *(Jim Parker)*

CP 57684 XM series 57525-58024
▲The 57684 is one of 500 cars built in 1960 by National Steel Car. It has NSC type 3 ends, Pullman-Standard type roof, Youngstown 8' door, interior height of 10'6" and a capacity of 3900 cu. ft. These cars were delivered in the stepped gothic lettering. Toronto, Ontario. March 5, 1988. *(John Riddell)*

CP 57710 XM series 57525-58024
▼National Steel Car built CP 57710 as one of 500 cars built in 1960. It has NSC type-3 ends, Pullman-Standard type roof, 8' Youngstown doors and a capacity of 3900 cu. ft. Agincourt, Ontario. November 1971. *(Jim Parker)*

CP 70179 XL series 70000-70198
◀Canadian Car and Foundry built this car in 1957 as series 53200-54199. This car has 10'6" interior height, improved dreadnaught ends, Superior 8' ribbed door, diagonal panel roof and 3900 cu. ft. It has movable bulkheads for securing lading and was painted two months before this view. Toronto, Ontario. April 1968. *(Jim Parker)*

CP 58702 XM series 58475-59174
▲This view of CP 58702 in Agincourt Yard Toronto in June 1970 clearly shows its Pullman-Standard type roof and NSC type 3 ends. It is one of 700 cars built in 1961 by National Steel Car. It has an Ajax handbrake, 8' Youngstown door, inside height of 10'6" and capacity of 3900 cu. ft. The Action Green paint scheme and shield indicate newsprint service. Agincourt Yard, Toronto. June 1970.
(Jim Parker)

CP 58896 XM series 58475-59174
▼Seen in Council Bluffs, Iowa on June 28, 1970, CP 58896 is one of 700 cars built in 1961 by National Steel Car. It has NSC type 3 ends, Pullman-Standard type roof, Ajax handbrake, 8' Youngstown door. The inside height is 10'6" and capacity is 3900 cu. ft. The Action Green paint scheme and shield indicate newsprint service. Council Bluffs, Iowa. June 28, 1970. *(Lou Schmitz)*

CP 70021 XL series 70000-70198
▲ The black symbol on the door indicates this car has moveable bulkheads for securing lading. The car has improved dreadnaught ends, Superior 8' ribbed door, capacity of 3549 cu. ft. and has had its running boards removed. Toronto, Ontario. October 3, 1985. *(Ronald Plazzotta)*

CP 23009 XM series 23000-23499
◀ Freshly shopped with running boards removed and cut-down ladders 23009 is seen in Agincourt Yard, Toronto in July 1977. It was built in 1955 by Canadian Car and Foundry as series 141700-142199. These were the only Canadian-built CP boxcars with 5-panel 6' Superior doors. It has improved dreadnaught ends, a diagonal panel roof and a capacity of 3900 cu. ft. *(Jim Parker)*

CP 49011 XL series 49010-49014
▼ CP 49011 is one of five cars for carrying asphalt shingles. It has moveable bulkheads and DF-1 belt rails. Stencil to left of door indicates WHEN EMPTY RETURN TO LASALLE QUEBEC. CP Rail Action Yellow was usually applied to insulated boxcars. The side sill is black. It was built in 1957 by Canadian Car and Foundry in series 53200-54199. It has Superior 8' ribbed doors, interior height 10'-6", 3229 cu. ft. capacity, running boards removed and low-height ladders. Toronto, Ontario. May 21, 1984.

(Gary R. Zuters)

INTERNATIONAL of MAINE

CP 269548 XM series 269100-269599
▲Pullman-Standard built this PS-1 boxcar in 1952-53 in the U.S. for the International of Maine division of the CP. It has PS-1 ends and roof, Ajax handbrake, Youngstown 6' doors and 3903 cu. ft. capacity. This car carries its original lettering. Four lettering schemes were applied to these cars: this single line scheme, stepped gothic, script and CP Rail lettering. Each scheme included INTERNATIONAL OF MAINE in small lettering. Agincourt Yard, Toronto. October 30, 1983. *(John Riddell)*

CP 269081 XM series 268800-269099
▶One of 300 PS-1 boxcars built in 1952 by Pullman-Standard, this car has PS-1 ends and roof, Ajax handbrake, Superior 5-panel 6' doors and a capacity of 3903 cu. ft. This car carries the script lettering. Agincourt Yard, Toronto. April 1982. *(Ken Grist)*

CP 23579 XM Ex-series 269800-269099
▼In June 1988 CP 23579G was in Leaside Yard, Toronto. One of 300 PS-1 boxcars built in 1952 by Pullman-Standard, it has PS-1 ends and roof, Ajax handbrake and Superior 5-panel 6' doors. The running boards have been removed and the ladders cut down. It has a CP Rail paint scheme.
(John Slean)

XMI BOXCARS

CP 35319 XMIH series 35000-35500
▲AAR class XMIH indicates a general service insulated and heated boxcar. It has 3 in. thick insulation and two underslung charcoal heaters and two heating coils in the car interior. CP 35319 has a 6' Superior rolling plug door. The car and was built 1959 by National Steel Car and still has its original stepped gothic lettering, although the running boards have been removed and ladders cut down and the paint has worn off the galvanized roof. The capacity is 3377 cu. ft. Agincourt Yard, Toronto. October 1979. *(Ken Grist)*

CP 36075 XIH series 35501-36100
▼This 50-ton insulated and heated boxcar was built by Hawker Siddeley, Trenton, Nova Scotia, formerly Eastern Car Company, in December 1963. It has a thermostatically controlled underslung alcohol heater and retains its original script lettering in Agincourt Yard, Toronto in May 1967. The capacity is 3458 cu. ft. *(Jim Parker)*

CP 35087 XMI series 35000-35500

▲Freshly painted in CP Rail Action Yellow, CP 35087 is shown in Agincourt Yard, Toronto in September 1969. It is equipped with an underslung charcoal heater. The long operating levers attached to short cams which engage in keepers at the top and bottom of the doors provide considerable leverage to close the door. The capacity is 3377 cu. ft. *(Jim Parker)*

CP 35893 XMI series 35501-36100

▼On November 28, 1978, using a specially assembled solid train CP Rail handled one of its largest single produce shipments. The special train, nicknamed the "Mandarin Orange Express" transported nearly 8 million Japanese oranges from Vancouver to various destinations accross Canada using 58 temperature-controlled boxcars. To advertise the shipment, insulated boxcar #35893 was painted in this unique Mandarin Express orange, black and white paint scheme. This car had been built in October 1962 and rebuilt in March 1978. Toronto, Ontario. January 1, 1986. *(John Riddell)*

40' GRAIN CARS

CP 143145 XM series 143000-143249
▲This grain car was painted in the CP Rail scheme in October 1978 at Weston shops, Winnipeg. The yellow doors for grain loading and inspection eliminate the need for inside grain doors as used in standard boxcars. Workers loading and unloading grain are provided with the ladder left of the door and narrow platform and grab irons on the door. The door latch is broken and a shim is being used to keep the plug door closed. Capacity is 3900 cubic feet. Agincourt Yard, Toronto. November 1979. *(Ken Grist)*

CP 143074 XM series 143000-143249
▼This view shows the roof of a 40' grain boxcar with its metal running board. It was built November 1955 and carries script lettering when photographed in Agincourt Yard, Toronto in September 1975. Capacity is 3900 cu. ft. *(Jim Parker)*

PLUG-SLIDING DOORS

CP 100197 XM series 100000-100499
▲The combination of a 6' plug door and 8' sliding door provides a more versatile car than a single door. The staggered 14' wide door openings facilitate the shipment of lumber, other bulky and palletized products and the mechanized loading and unloading of these commodities. Built by National Steel Car in 1962 the car's roof paint has worn from its galvanized roof. Capacity is 3900 cu. ft. Smiths Falls, Ontario. March 1976. *(Tom Hood)*

CP 100097 XM series 100000-100499
▼When a single-door car is required, the 6' plug door is closed and locked. The running boards had been removed and ladders cut down when the car was photographed in Thunder Bay, Ontario in August 18, 1984. Car capacity is 3900 cu. ft.
(Ronald A. Plazzotta)

DOUBLE-DOOR

CP 296639 XM series 296639-296709
▲This automobile car has a 15' side-door opening, 9'-2" wide end-door and capacity of 3898 cu. ft. This, the first car of a series of 70 built in November 1951, still had its original lettering when photographed at Cranbrook, British Columbia in July 1979. *(John Riddell)*

CP 299454 XH series 299401-299599
▼The height has been raised, doors widened and side-sill strengthened on this automobile car seen at Smiths Falls, Ontario in April 1969. It does not have an end door. The capacity is 3898 cu. ft. *(Tom Hood)*

CP 291626 XM series 291500-291799
▲This automobile car has staggered 15'-0" door openings and a full width door in the 'A' end. The inside length is 40'-6" and capacity is 3890 cu. ft. Agincourt Yard, Toronto. July 11, 1981. *(John Riddell)*

EN 292352 XM series 292000-292384
▼In January 1983, of the 455 40' boxcars lettered for the Esquimalt & Nanaimo Railway, a CP subsidiary on Vancouver Island, 374 were cars like this one. CP had purchased the E&N in 1905 and absorbed it into the CP system. In 1978 CP started painting boxcars in E&N lettering, possibly for tax purposes. This car was relettered in 1982 but kept its original CP number. Capacity is 3895 cu. ft. Agincourt Yard, Toronto. October 9, 1983. *(John Riddell)*

50' BOX CARS

CP 78000 XM series 78000-78014
▲This car, the first of the series built in December 1964 by Hawker-Siddeley, carries the NEWSPRINT SERVICE ONLY red shield logo. These cars carry newsprint in large rolls, stacked on end in two tiers. The 9'-wide plug-door has single vertical rods for locking. Capacity is 5090 cu. ft. Toronto, July 7, 1979. *(John Slean)*

CP 80580 XM series 80000-80966
◀CP 80580 is a 70-ton boxcar for newsprint service. It has an outside length of 57'-10", 9'-wide plug-door, cushion underframe, nailable steel floor. It was built by Hawker-Siddeley in April 1965. The 'Superior' plug door has double vertical rods for locking. Capacity is 5090 cu. ft. Dimensional data has not been stencilled below the shield as is usual. Hornell NY, September 1966. *(Jim Parker)*

CP 81005 XM series 80967-81216
▼Built by National Steel Car in 1967, this 70-ton boxcar carries the green scheme with pine tree herald indicating newsprint service. It has a 57'-10" outside length, 9'-wide plug-door, cushion underframe and nailable steel floor. Capacity is 5090 cu. ft. Agincourt, Ontario. August 21, 1984. *(Ronald Plazzotta)*

CP 81046 XM series 80967-81216
▶This view in Agincourt Yard, Toronto in April 1974 shows the roof and end of another newsprint car in its original paint scheme, the pine tree herald. This Plate C car was built in April 1967 by National Steel Car without running boards nor full-height ladders. The ends and side sills are black. *(Jim Parker)*

CP 84981 XP series 84977-84999
▼When some newsprint was made in wider rolls, the rolls could not be double-stacked in the regular cars so 22 cars were rebuilt with increased height. The 11'-11" interior height cars exceeded standard height and exceeded Plate C clearance. An AAR Plate clearance diagram defines the dimensional clearances that a car meets. The inside length was 50'6". The car was built in April 1967 by National Steel Car and rebuilt in 1981. Toronto, Ontario. October 26, 1987. *(Gary R. Zuters)*

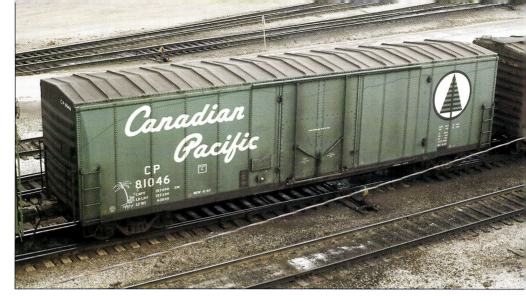

CP 80898 XM series 80000-80966
▼This is another 70-ton newsprint car in Fremont Nebraska on February 24, 1974. The CP Rail logo is 24" high and 9'-8 " long and starts 3'-11 " from the car's 'A'-end and 7' above the car side sill. The reporting marks are 10". The black and white multimark logo is at the car's 'B'-end on both sides. *(Lou Schmitz)*

CPI 85079 XM series 85000-85499
▲CP cars bearing reporting mark 'CPI' are Canadian-built cars restricted to international service between Canada and the United States and must not be used in domestic service in either country. This is for tax considerations. Similarly reporting mark 'CPAA' indicates a US-built car restricted to international service. Built by National Steel Car, #85079 is four months old and has a capacity of 5140 cubic feet, 9'-0" plug door and a cushioned underframe. Agincourt, Ontario. September 1969. *(Jim Parker)*

CPI 85167 XM series 85000-85499
▼The CP Rail logo is 24" high and 9'-8" long and starts 3'-4" from the car's A-end and 7' above the car side sill. The reporting marks are 10" white and the small dimensional lettering is 3" black. Green is used to denote cars in newsprint service. CPI 85167 was built by National Steel Car in May 1969. Marion, Ohio. August 1971. *(Paul C. Winters)*

CPI 85594 XP series 85500-85634
◄This view shows the roof and end of a 70-ton newsprint car. It has an inside length of 50'6", a 10'-wide plug-door and a cushion underframe. It was built by National Steel Car in May 1975. Agincourt, Ontario. September 1975.
(Jim Parker)

CPI 85719 XP series 85635-85734

▲Photographed new at Burlington, Ontario on October 30 1977 is this 70-ton exterior-post newsprint car. It has an inside length of 50'6", 9'-wide Camel plug-door, ACF Freightsaver cushion underframe with 20" travel, nailable steel floor. The white shield indicates "Newsprint Service Only". Built by National Steel Car. This car meets AAR Plate C clearance and has a capacity of 5111 cu. ft. *(Gary R. Zuters)*

**CP 293691 XMR
series 293435-293934**

▲Note the two shades of mineral red on the two automobile boxcars. CP 293691 has an inside length of 50'6" and a combination sliding main door and plug door for its 16' door opening. The car is equipped with Evans auto loading racks as indicated by the white door stripe. When configured for auto loading, the capacity is 4860 cu. ft. and with devices stored, the capacity is 4360 cu. ft. Built by NSC in 1959, it has its original stepped gothic lettering. On the left is CP 294615. Toronto, Ontario. May 1960. *(Jim Parker)*

**CP 293822 XMR
series 293435-293934**

▼This automobile car in Oshawa Ontario in June 1963 is equipped with Evans loading racks for loading automobiles and is also suitable for general service loading of other miscellaneous commodities. Stencil to left of the door states TO BE USED EXCLUSIVELY FOR NEWSPRINT PAPER FLOUR AND SUGAR OR OTHER HIGH CLASS MERCHANDISE. *(Jim Parker)*

CP 42603 XP series 42602-42611
▲CP 42603 is adapted for automobile parts - auto springs in racks. It has a nailable steel floor, inside length of 45'10" and a 16'-wide door opening. It was built in July 1962 and has a capacity of 4410 cu. ft. The white panel indicates the car is for GM AUTO SPRINGS. The car was built by Hawker-Siddeley Trenton Works as series 200000-098. Agincourt Yard, Toronto February 20, 1983. *(John Riddell)*

CP 42620 XP series 42618-42629
▼CP has long served large automobile plants of General Motors in Oshawa, Ontario and Ford in Oakville, Ontario. CP 42620 has two 8'-wide centered sliding doors, DF-1 belt rails, cross members to accomodate auto stampings and a capacity of 4865 cu. ft. The white panel indicates GM ASSIGNED SERVICE OSHAWA. The car has full-height ladders but the running board has been removed. Each door is equipped with a Hennessy Door Control which uses the rolling leverage of the wheel to move the door via a cog on the rack. #42620 was built in 1952 as series 199000-077. Oshawa, Ontario. July 10, 1980. *(John Slean)*

CP 42633 XL series 42632-42634
▼In July 1979, CP owned 53 different series of boxcars specially equipped for automobile parts. This is one of three cars for auto brake drums. It has DF-1 belt rails installed. Its outside length is 54'4" and it has two 8'-wide centered sliding doors and capacity of 4866 cu. ft. The large script herald applied left of doors is unusual. White panel requests that the car RETURN TO WOODSTOCK ONTARIO. Agincourt Yard, Toronto. June 1972.
(John Slean)

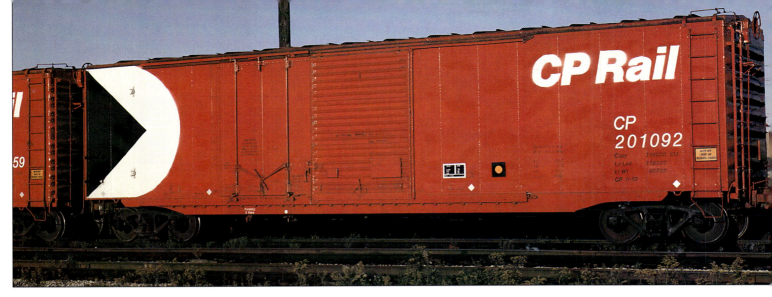

CP 201092 XM series 201000-201494
▲Freshly painted less than a month before in CP Rail scheme, #201092 is seen in Agincourt Yard, Toronto on October 9, 1983. The 50-ton car is wood-lined, has a 50'6" inside length and 16'-wide staggered combination plug and sliding doors. It was built in 1959 as series 293000 with a capacity of 4860 cu. ft. *(John Riddell)*

CP 202132 XM series 202000-202199
▼On August 18, 1984, #202132 was rolling through Thunder Bay Ontario when photographed. It is wood-lined and has an inside length of 50'-6". The 16'-wide staggered door openings have combination plug and sliding doors. The capacity is 4870 cu. ft. *(Ronald Plazzotta)*

CP 202248 XM series 202200-202449
▼This series of 50'6" boxcars was converted from standard 40' boxcars in 1968-69. It has an inside length of 50'6" and staggered doors over a 16' opening. Capacity is 4926 cu. ft. Agincourt, Ontario. October 1974. *(Jim Parker)*

CP 204049 XM series 204000-204139
▲This is one of 140 similar exterior-post boxcars built by National Steel Car in 1974. It has an inside length of 50'8" and 18'-wide staggered door openings and flat ends. The two 9' sliding plug doors are flush gear operated. It has 33" diameter wheels in roller bearing trucks and a capacity of 5380 cu. ft. or 152,000 lbs. Agincourt, Ontario. June 19, 1983. *(John Slean)*

CP 166195 XLIH series 166000-166199
▼National Steel Car built 200 of these insulated heated boxcars in 1966. It has 3" insulation and a thermostatically-controlled underslung alcohol heater for a vapour floor-heat system. The sliding plug doors are 9'-wide and 9'-high. Moveable bulkheads are installed inside. The capacity is 3970 cu. ft. and the inside length is 49'8". It has a cushion underframe. Orange and black were the standard colors of insulated heated boxcars prior to CP Rail yellow. January 1968. Toronto, Ontario. *(Jim Parker)*

60' BOX CARS

CP 166577 XLIH series 166549-166592

▲This car was painted less than a month before this photo in Agincourt Yard, Toronto on August 3, 1981. Insulated heated box car 166577 was built by National Steel Car in March 1972. It has sliding plug doors for the 12'0"-wide by 9'-9" high door openings. A thermostatically-controlled underslung alcohol heater feeds a vapour floor heat system. It has moveable bulkheads, an inside length of 50'7" and a capacity of 4526 cu. ft.

(John Slean)

CP 205518 XAP series 205500-205625

▼This is one of 126 70-ton boxcars built by Pullman-Standard in its Michigan City, Indiana plant in 1966. It is used for shipping automobile stampings from auto plants in the U.S. to assemply plants in Ontario. It has a Hydroframe-40 cushion underframe, DF-1 belt rails, steel floor, sliding doors 10' wide by 11' high. The cars have an inside length of 60'-9" and a capacity of 6344 cubic feet. Since the car was built in the U.S. it carries the International of Maine Division lettering indicating it is permitted under U.S. customs regulations to be used in the same manner as cars bearing U.S. railway reporting marks in the handling of international and U.S. domestic traffic. The cars would rarely, if ever, be on the Maine Division. The white panel indicates "Return Empty to NYC RR at Collingwood Ohio". Agincourt, Ontario. May 1967. *(Jim Parker)*

 ## Refrigerator Cars

CP 288936 RSM series 288500-288999
▲This wood freight ice reefer is equipped with rails for hanging beef. It has divided-basket ice bunkers and a 'liquidometer' temperature indicating apparatus. A charcoal heater is beneath the door. The number has been painted over indicating the car is officially removed from the company roster. Hinged doors close the 5' wide x 6'-4" tall openings. It was built in June 1930 and was last weighed at Angus Shops in February 1952. Capacity is 1975 cu. ft. Ottawa West, 1954. *(Graham Stremes)*

CP 288964 RSM series 288500-288999
◄Wood freight ice reefer #288964 is awaiting scrapping at Morley, Alberta in January 1969. It has divided-basket ice bunkers and a liquidometer temperature indicating apparatus. Charcoal heater is beneath the door. The number has been painted over indicating the car is officially removed from the company roster. Capacity is 1975 cu. ft.
(John Riddell)

CP 450211 WY series 450000-450999
▼This wood freight ice reefer carries a company service number. It has four roof hatches open to the end ice bunkers. Hinged doors cover the 4' wide x 6'-4" opening. It was built in April 1931 as series 289000-289249 and has a capacity of 1975 cu. ft. The car is in company ice service as indicated by class WY. Smiths Falls, Ontario. May 1969.
(Tom Hood)

CP 281310 RAMH series 281001-282398

▶CP took delivery of 3,102 8-hatch steel freight reefers from 1936 to 1956. They were assigned sixteen number series. This car was built by National Steel Car Co. in March 1946 and is a brine-tank refrigerator with meat rails. This view shows the stepped gothic lettering scheme. The charcoal-fuelled heater mounted beneath the door was used during cold weather to protect shipments from freezing while the ice bunkers were used in the summer for cooling. The liquidometer temperature gauge is below 'M' stencil. The door opening is 5' wide and 6'-8" high and is closed by hinged doors. Capacity is 2268 cu. ft. A number of these cars were equipped for passenger train service. These cars were delivered in the Spans-the-World lettering. September 1959. Windsor, Ontario. *(Emery J. Gulash)*

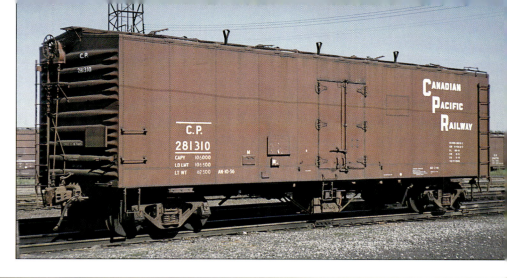

CP 281312 RAMH series 281001-282398

▲CP 8-hatch reefers had several different hatch-opening configurations. This car has its eight roof hatches hinged on their sides nearest the roof center. The six uprights support the hatches when in their open position. Each hatch lead to a separate shallow overhead ice tank, with a capacity of 6,500 pounds of ice. The overhead tanks avoided the conventional end ice bunkers and allowed more space for revenue loading. The capacity is 2268 cu. ft. or 104000 lbs. It has a steel mesh roof walk. CP 281312 has had some recent repairs to its door which has been repainted. It was built in March 1946. Canadian National had slightly different 8-hatch steel reefers - gray CN 210248 is coupled to the right. December 1962. Columbus, Ohio.

(Paul C. Winters)

CP 401448 RAMH ex-series 283300-283499

▶Series 283300-283499 of 8-hatch freight reefers had plug doors for their 5' x 6'-8" opening. Capacity is 2268 cu. ft. Different series of 8-hatched reefers had numerous major variations such as types of doors, ends, roof walks, heaters and brake wheels. It was built by NSC in April 1953. In 1965, 2,951 were still in service but by 1972 only 346 remained. This reefer, in Calgary in April 1974, has been renumbered with a service number and carries the script lettering scheme.

(John Riddell)

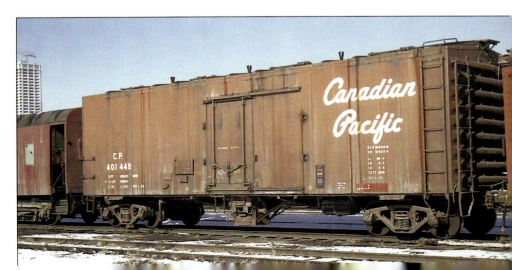

CP 285606 RPL series 285600-285614
▲This is one of 15 cars rebuilt in 1963 as mechanical refrigerator cars on which the heating and refrigeration systems have since been de-activated. It has two one-piece moveable bulkheads and plug door openings of 8'-0" x 8'-11". The fuel tank is below door. Capacity is 3230 cu. ft. It is silver with large red script and black reporting marks. Fredericton, New Brunswick. 1970. *(Gordon Jomini)*

CP 286266 RPM series 286135-286279
◄CP 286266 is a mechanical reefer with meat rails for hanging beef. It has an exterior length of 55'-5" and a capacity of 3294 cubic feet. It has no running boards and refrigeration equipment is mounted in the A-end of car. It has silver sides and roof, black ends and side sills. The red script lettering was later replaced by CP Rail lettering. The car was built by National Steel Car in 1967. July 8, 1982. Agincourt Yard, Ontario.
(John Slean)

CP 287217 RPL series 287207-287256
▼This mechanical reefer with meat rails has an outside length of 55'-5" and a capacity of 3194 cubic feet. The Multimark is at the cars B end and refrigeration equipment is in the A end. The car was built in 1967 by National Steel Car. August 21, 1983. Calgary, Alberta.
(Ronald A. Plazzotta)

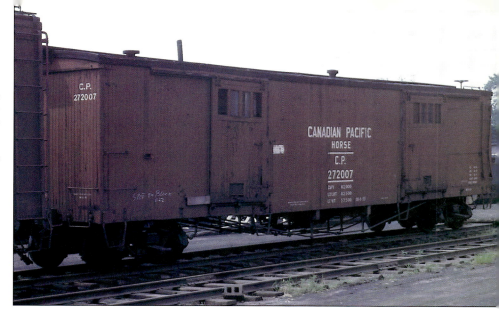

CP 272007 SC series 272000-272013
▶CP had at least three types of horse cars. This is one of 14 all-wood 40-ton horse cars equipped with 16 collapsible steel stalls and feed troughs. On each side are two sliding wood doors - the left door is 5'-wide, the right is 6'-wide. Both doors are 7'-7" high. The inside length is 46'-1". It has four truss-rods, arch-bar trucks and K brakes. Two smoke jacks indicate heating stoves. This car was built in October 1913 as series 257983-257999. It is freight car red with a black roof. Capacity is 3003 cu. ft. Agincourt yard, Toronto. July 1967. *(Jim Parker)*

 ## Stock Cars

CP 272014 SC series 272014-272028
▶This car was built in April 1928 as series 258000-258014. It is one of 15 all-steel 40-ton horse cars equipped with 16 collapsible steel stalls. The inside length is 46'-0". It has flat ends. On each side are two 6'-wide sliding wood doors, 8'-8" high. It has a radial roof. The number is painted over indicating it has been removed from the roster. Some of these horse cars received the CP Rail paint scheme. Capacity is 3795 cu. ft. Assiniboia Downs racetrack, Winnipeg. September 1992. *(Brian Schuff)*

CP 279912 SM series 279800-279999
▼CP converted some 4,200 of its 33,000 Fowler-patent 36' boxcars into stock cars between 1919 and 1965. These were typical of CP stock cars into the 1960's. #279912 was rebuilt between 1959 and 1965. It has a 5' door, AB brakes and a capacity of 2448 cu. ft. In 1955, 2,800 of these stock cars remained in revenue service. In 1965, 890 were still on the roster. Keith, Alberta. August 1968. *(John Riddell)*

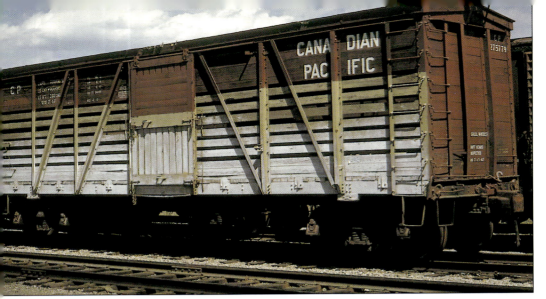

CP 275779 SM series 274500-276899
◀ CP 275779 was built in April 1913 as a boxcar and was rebuilt into a stock car between 1936 and 1945. It has a capacity of 3664 cu. ft. and was last weighed at Weston shops Winnipeg in July 1967. The white sides have a coat of lime disinfectant. The number has been painted over indicating the car is to be scrapped at Ogden Shops, Alberta, June 1969.
(John Riddell)

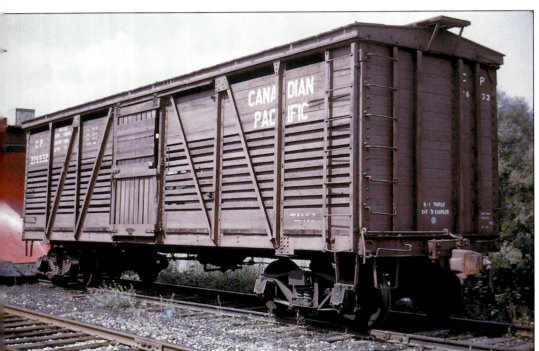

CP 276932 SM series 276900-276987
◀ CP 276932 was formerly CP subsidiary Quebec Central Railway #2266. In 1951 the QC had 230 such 36' Fowler stock cars in service. Many QC stock cars had thinner slats than the CP cars. When photographed at Preston, Ontario in August 1962, #276932 retained its original archbar trucks and K brakes. It is brown over-all with neither white paint nor lime disinfectant. Capacity is 2448 cu. ft.
(Don McQueen Collection)

CP 277083 SM series 277000-277199
▼ CP 277083 was rebuilt from a steel boxcar that had been built in March 1958. CP sold this car to a cattle auction market and it was being used to ship livestock from Fort Macleod, Alberta to Toronto when it was photographed in Agincourt Yard, Toronto on June 11, 1980. The placard indicates Double deck owned by Fort Macleod Auction Market. Return to Fort Macleod. It was last reweighed at St. Luc yard Montreal in June 1969. Capacity is 3863 cu. ft. *(John Riddell)*

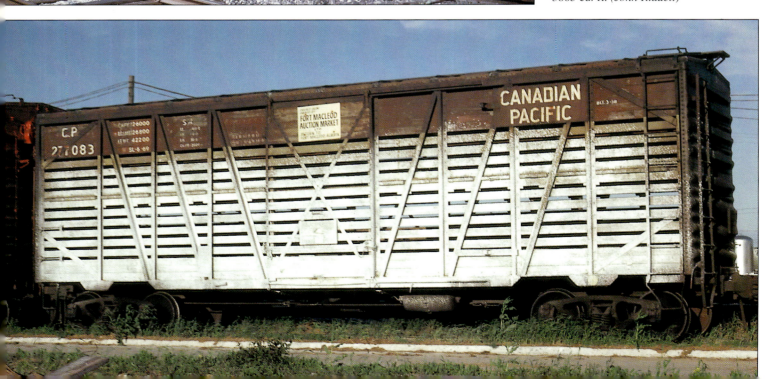

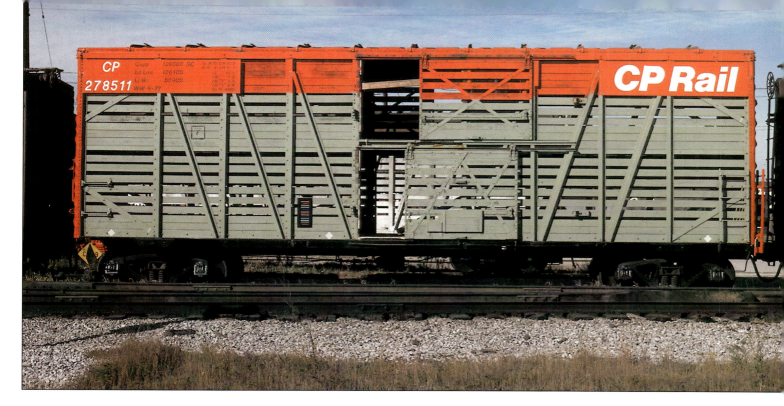

CP 278511 SC
series 278500-278531
▲This double-deck stock car has an inside length of 40'-6", lower deck height of 5'-4" and upper deck height of 4'-11". The two doors are 6' wide and 4'-11" high. It was rebuilt from a boxcar in Winnipeg in September 1977, only a month before this photo. It carries CP Rail action red, grey slats, black sidesill and trucks. It has triangular reflectors. Capacity is 4080 cu. ft. Agincourt yard, Toronto. October 29, 1977. *(Gary R. Zuters)*

CP 277111 SC
series 277000-277199
▶This is one of 45 CP stock cars equipped with a semi-permanent steel upper deck, conventional sliding doors for the lower deck and two-piece sliding doors for the upper-deck. Capacity is 3863 cu. ft. Built in 1958, this car is now preserved in the Henry Ford Museum in Dearborn, Michigan. Agincourt Yard, Toronto. April 11, 1992. *(John Riddell)*

CP 277713 SM
series 277500-277870
▶In July 1943 during World War II CP purchased 500 boxcars, series 223950-224449, from Canadian Car and Foundry. These had sides single-sheathed with 5/8" plywood and 1/4" plywood rooves to reduce steel consumption during wartime. In 1958-59 351 of the 500 boxcars were converted to stock cars such as #277713. It has a rectangular panel roof and five panels on each side of the 6' door. The interior height is 10'-6" and capacity is 3664 cu. ft. Calgary, Alberta. July 1981. *(Tom Hood)*

PICTURE-WINDOW STOCK CARS

CP 278154 SM
series 278001-278299

◀ In June 1966 stock car 278154 was converted in Weston shops from a steel radial-roof boxcar, series 225000-225699, built in February 1936. When photographed in Agincourt Yard, Toronto it is only one month old. It is a 40-ton single-deck stockcar with 5'9"-wide sliding doors, inside length of 40'-6" and inside height of 9'-4". Capacity is 3249 cu. ft. It is freight car red with grey slats and has four diamond-shaped reflectors. Agincourt Yard, Toronto. July 1966. *(Jim Parker)*

CP 278224 SM
series 278001-278299

◀ This stock car has a coat of lime wash disinfectant. The CP Rail logo is at the 'B' car end. These were sometimes described as 'picture window' stock cars due to the large openings cut in the steel sides. These cars were converted in 1965-67 from boxcars built in 1936. Agincourt Yard, Toronto. October 30, 1983.

(John Riddell)

CP 278252 SM
series 278001-278299

▼CP 278252 was rebuilt in Weston shops in April 1967 from a steel boxcar built in February 1936. It has a lime wash and its running board has been removed from the roof. In January 1977, 270 of this series of stock cars were in service. In January 1983, 181 were still in service. Smiths Falls, Ontario. May 1969.

(Tom Hood)

Open Hoppers

CP 357156 HM series 357000-357249
▲Built in November 1941 #357156 was a two-bay hopper of 2190 cu. ft. capacity. CP painted its open top hoppers and gondolas black with 9" white lettering. In 1951 1,149 such hoppers were in service. By 1965, 1,125 were still left. Revelstoke, B.C. June 1967. *(Jim Parker)*

CP 354127 HM series 354000-354899
▼In June 1967 #354127 was in Revelstoke, B.C. when photographed. It was built in April 1937 by National Steel Car with Yost hopper doors. The bottom of the side has been repaired with a replacement panel. It carries script lettering which was likely applied when it was refurbished in Angus Shops in December 1966. Prior to acquiring these twin hoppers, CP shipped coal in high-side gondolas. *(Jim Parker)*

CP 354517 HM series 354000-354899
▶Built in May 1938 twin hopper #354517 has Yost hopper doors. It is unlikely that any of these twin hoppers received CP Rail multimark lettering. Smiths Falls, Ontario. January 1972.
(Tom Hood)

**CP 354839 HM
series 354000-354899**
▲This hopper has been loaded at Canmore Mines and is spotted in the yard at Canmore, Alberta in the front range of the Rockies, to be picked up by the CP. May 1976. *(John Riddell)*

CP 364397 HT series 364000-364974
▼CP operated unit coal trains from Coleman Collieries at Coleman, Alberta to Port Moody B.C. during the 1966-1967 period. A fleet of 80-ton triple hoppers was assigned and stenciled with a white panel with black letters COLEMAN — PORT MOODY. Below in smaller white letters was COAL SERVICE. These were later replaced by bathtub gons. This damaged car awaits scrapping at Ogden Shops, Calgary. October 1974. #364397 was built by National Steel Car in 1958 and has a capacity of 2775 cu. ft.
(John Riddell)

CP 357669 HT series 357450-357999
▲CP triple hoppers had two orientations of the hopper doors. On some cars two doors opened toward the cars 'B' end - on others only one. CP 357669 has only one door opening to the 'B' end. The car has a capacity 2773 cu. ft. or 80 tons and was built in October 1956 by National Steel Car. Agincourt Yard, Toronto. September 30, 1978. *(Gary R. Zuters)*

CP 357769 HT series 357450-357999
▲On October 9, 1983, triple #357769 was in Agincourt Yard Toronto when photographed. It carries script lettering. The large 'P' indicates the car was assigned to a pool. In July 1965, 4,655 such triple hoppers were in service. By January 1983 1,931 were in service. *(John Riddell)*

CP 358713 HT series 358600-358949
▼This triple hopper has two hopper doors facing the 'B' car end. The large multimark extends to the top of the side. The car was built in 1953 by the Eastern Car Company, Trenton, Nova Scotia and has a capacity of 2775 cu. ft. Agincourt Yard, Toronto. September 30, 1978. *(Gary R. Zuters)*

CP 361073 HK series 360200-361227
▲This car with longitudinal hoppers for dumping its contents under the car and/or outside the rails is intended primarily for track ballasting service. Longitudinal hoppers are also useful for handling bulk commodities subject to freezing since the large side doors make the lading easily accessible. It was built in November 1953 and has a capacity of 2775 cu. ft. Quebec Street Yard, London, Ontario, October 1, 1988. *(Don McQueen)*

CP 360367 HK series 360200-361227
▼Built by Eastern Car Co. in January 1952 this 70-ton longitudinal hopper car has four side doors, four center doors and the Enterprise Door Operating Mechanism. The four side doors are controlled from the ends of the car and the center doors from either side at the center of the car. Quebec Street Yard, London, Ontario, November 2, 1980. *(Don McQueen)*

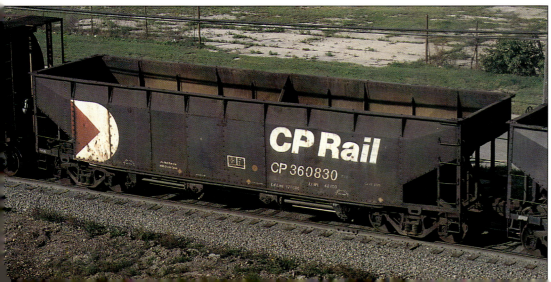

CP 360830 HK series 360200-361227
◀This ballast car has four longitudinal hoppers for dumping the ballast contents under the car and/or outside the rails. Each hopper has two openings of 5'-2" X 2'-7" with two doors hinged length-wise to direct the flow as required. It is intended primarily for track ballasting service. A small multimark is only on the flat vertical side. It was built in 1953. Winnipeg, Manitoba, September 24, 1994.

(F. Headon)

 Covered Hoppers

SLAB-SIDE HOPPERS

CP 380175 LO series 380001-380700
▲National Steel Car built this 3000 cubic foot hopper in 1948. It has 10 hatches (two 5' X 3' center hatches and eight 3' X 3') and eight outlet gates. The length over end sills is 41'-7". CP owned a total of 1,473 slab side hoppers - 910 with six hatches. CP 380175 had script lettering when photographed in Agincourt Yard, Ontario in September 1975. *(Jim Parker)*

CP 380212 LO series 380001-380700
▼Seen in Marion, Ohio in July 1963, CP 380212 has six rectangular hatches and eight 13"x24" outlet gates. Built in August 1950 by National Steel Car it has four compartments and carries its original 9" gothic lettering. The stencil indicates Assigned Syenite Service When Empty Return to Havelock Ont. All CP 'slabside' hoppers had open side sills. *(Paul C. Winters)*

CP 385801 LO series 385000-385019
▲Originally built in 1958 by Marine Industries Ltd., this is one of 200 cars upgraded in 1961 with 100-ton trucks and reinforced end-bracing for cement service. It has six hatches on a smooth roof and eight outlet gates. The length over end sills is 41'-7" and the capacity is 3000 cu. ft. The multimark is at 'B' car end as usual. For more information refer to an article in the August 1986 issue of *Railroad Model Craftsman* magazine. Marion, Ohio. July 1963. *(Paul C. Winters)*

CP 380690 LO series 380001-380700
▼Built by National Steel Car in 1953, CP 380690 has six hatches and eight outlet gates. The length over end sills is 41'-7". The Multimark is on the A car end which is unusual. Leaside yard, Toronto. November 3, 1991. *(John Slean)*

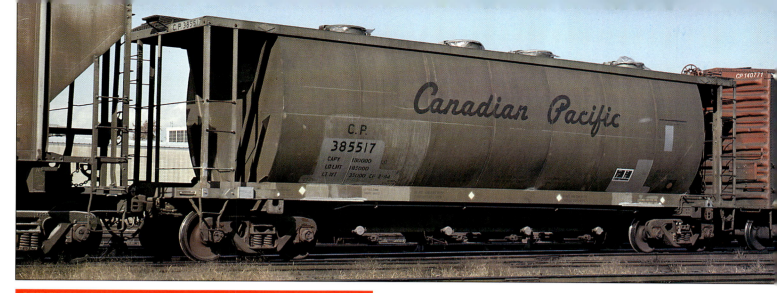

CYLINDRICAL

CP 385517 LO series 385500-385553
▲This aluminum hopper has a flat roof with 8 cylindrical hatches - four on each side of the running board. It has four 24" X 13" gravity gates with auxillary 4"-diameter pneumatic outlets. The capacity is 3000 cu. ft. and the outside length is 47'7". This is one of 250 aluminum cars built by the National Steel Car in February 1964 as CP 383000-383249. Problems developed with corrosion and metal fatigue at welded seams and stress points. Only 53 cars still operated in January 1983. The black script lettering is on unpainted aluminum. Toronto, Ontario. September 21, 1984.
(Ronald Plazzotta)

CP 386762 LO series 386000-386889
▲This steel 3400 cubic foot hopper has eight 30"-diameter cylindrical hatches and four sliding outlet gates. The outside length is 49'9". The series was built in 1964-65 by National Steel Car. Agincourt Yard, Toronto. June 19, 1983. *(John Slean)*

CP 384412 LO series 384000-384499
▼National Steel Car built this steel hopper in May 1966. It has four 30"-diameter hatches along the center of roof with a running board along each side. Four seperate epoxy-lined compartments are emptied by four center-discharge hopper outlets. The capacity is 3400 cubic feet and the outside length is 49'9". Toronto, Ontario. January 1968. *(Jim Parker)*

CP 385604 LO series 385600-385609
▲Marine Industries Limited built this steel hopper in Sorel Quebec in February 1967. It has a capacity of 3800 cubic feet and pneumatic outlets. These were normally used for dry bulk commodities such as potash, soda ash, fertilizer, cement, flour, sugar and salt rather than grain. Cobourg, Ontario. May 1978. *(Jim Walder, John Riddell Collection)*

CP 387463 LO series 387000-387599
▼Photographed in Windsor Ontario in November 1974, this hopper has four separate epoxy-lined compartments with a 33' trough loading hatch and four sliding outlet doors. It has a capacity of 3800 cubic feet and a length over strikers of 51'-8". It was built in 1968 by Hawker Siddeley Trenton Works. The white line indicates the maximum for cement loading. Windsor, Ontario. November 1974.
(Emery J. Gulash)

CP 385206 LO series 385100-385214
▼Built by National Steel Car in June 1977 this hopper has a capacity of 4550 cubic feet. Note that the Multimark extends down over side-sill. These cars were used primarily for grain service. Agincourt Yard, Toronto. July 1977. *(Jim Parker)*

**CP 382263 LO
series 382000-382499**

▲This steel hopper has a tear-drop design, four separate epoxy-lined compartments, four 30"-diameter centerline loading hatches, and four sliding outlet doors. The outside length is 53'10" and the capacity is 3800 cu. ft. It was built in 1966 by Marine Industries Limited and is painted aluminum. Agincourt Yard. May 27, 1977. *(Gary R. Zuters)*

**CP 381949 LO
series 381920-381959**

▶CP handled concentrated ore in slurry form in 60 covered hoppers with a length over strikers of 29'-5". Two compartments with two 5' long hatches provided a total capacity of 25 tons or 1600 cubic feet. #381949 has two quick-dump outlet doors and is shown in its first month of operation, November 1969, in Sudbury. These were used to ship ore slurry from the Falconbridge Ltd. mine at Onaping to its mill at Wanapitei. Some of these cars carried white script lettering. *(Jim McRae)*

**CP 381952 LO
series 381920-381959**

▶This slurry hopper was photographed in Toronto on August 21, 1988. It has two quick-dump outlet doors. These were built in October 1969 by Davie Ship Engineering. It has 36" diameter wheels.

(Gary R. Zuters)

PRESSURE DIFFERENTIAL COVERED HOPPERS

CP 381719 LO series 381700-381719
▲Pressure differential covered hoppers were designed for unloading bulk commodities requiring air pressures in the 1 to 14 psi range. CP 381719 is a 4-bay, positive pressure differential (PPD) hopper of a tear-drop design. It has a capacity of 2900 cu. ft. or 100 tons and an extreme length of 49'-11". These cars have a single epoxy-lined compartment, four centerline loading hatches and 4 in. diameter steel discharge piping equipped with Kamlok fittings. It was built in October 1966 by National Steel Car. It has silver sides with a black roof, ladders, underbody and lettering. This is one of two such cars fitted with stainless steel discharge piping and fittings to permit handling of edible commodities. Toronto, circa 1967. *(Jim Parker Collection)*

CP 381754 LO series 381728-381777
▼CP 381754 was designed for unloading bulk commodities such as dry caustic soda requiring air pressures in the 1 to 30 psi range. It has a steel cylindrical design with a capacity of 2928 cu. ft. or 100 tons and a length over strikers of 44'-5". These cars have a single epoxy-lined compartment. Loading is through three centerline 24" loading hatches spaced 12'-0" and unloading is through three 4-inch diameter steel discharge pipes equipped with Kamlok fittings. The car is not suitable for edible commodities. It has roller bearing trucks with 36" wheels and is silver overall. Built by PROCOR in Oakville Ontario in 1966, it is leased to CP. Toronto, Ontario. January 21, 1989. *(Gary R. Zuters)*

CP 381806 LO series 381800-381849
▲CP 381806 has a steel cylindrical 4-bay design with a capacity of 3800 cu. ft. or 100 ton cars. It has a length over strikers of 54'-2" and a height of 14'-2". It was designed for unloading bulk commodities requiring air pressures in the 1 to 30 psi range. The car was built in March 1969 by PROCOR which leased it to CP. Toronto, Ontario. November 27, 1988. *(Gary R. Zuters)*

CP 381837 LO series 381800-381849
▼CP 381837 has 4-bays with 4 hatches along center of roof with a walkway on each side. These cars have a single epoxy-lined compartment. Loading is through four centerline 24" hatches, spaced 10'-7", and unloading is by air through 4-inch diameter steel discharge piping equipped with Kamlok fittings. The roller bearing trucks have 36" wheels. It has silver sides, black roof, underbody and lettering. The car was built in June 1969 by PROCOR which leased it to CP. Toronto, Ontario. February 5, 1987. *(Gary R. Zuters)*

75

Ore Cars

CP 373??? HMB series 373001-373129
◄ This ore car is one of 65 cars built September 1907 as series 53001-53129 (odd numbers only). It has been retired with its number painted over and is hours away from being cut up in the scrap line at Ogden Shops, Calgary in 1969. It was one of only three surviving such cars at that date. It has a capacity of 725 cubic feet or 40 tons, an inside length of 22'-7" and six side ribs. These cars, commonly used in southern B.C., were some of the first steel freight cars owned by CP. Like other Canadian railways, before 1913 CP assigned odd numbers to its open-top cars and even numbers to its closed house cars. *(John Riddell)*

CP 375039 HMB series 375000-375399
▲ Shown in Nelson B.C. in July 1971, this is one of 164 cars with a capacity of 892 cubic feet or 50 tons and inside length of 26'-6". It has eight side ribs. It was designed and built by Dominion Car and Foundry, Montreal, in March 1908, in series 55001-55999 (odd numbers only). The white panel states THIS CAR MUST NOT BE LOADED FOR DESTINATIONS IN THE UNITED STATES. In July 1965, 63 such ore cars were still in service. *(Tom Hood)*

CP 375964 GT series 375900-375999
▼ Seen in Whitefish Ontario in October 1978, this is one of 100 cars built in March 1942 during World War II. It has a capacity of 1180 cubic feet. It was built as AAR class HMB, with drop-bottom doors that have since been welded closed creating a solid-bottom class GT car, locally called a 'tight bottom'. With the installation of a rotary dumper at INCO's gigantic Clarabelle Mill, the drop doors on many CP cars were welded shut. The dumper empties two ore cars at once. *(John Riddell)*

CP 370008 GS
series 370000-370124

▶ This is one of 125 cars built by Canadian Car and Foundry in 1916 for the Algoma Eastern Railway as series 2801-2925. CP leased the AER in 1930 and acquired its rolling stock. With script lettering, it has a temporary wood cover and is assigned to One Man Rock Service for the Engineering Department of the Sudbury Subdivision. Sudbury, Ontario. August 1975.

(Bryan Sirman)

CP 376970 GS
series 376900-376999

▶ Photographed at Whitefish Ontario in October 1978, #376970 was built in July 1956 and has a capacity of 1220 cubic feet. Unlike Canadian National, CP has never had a large traffic in iron ore. However CP has had a large traffic in non-ferrous ores and concentrates. In 1950 CP carried 4.3 million tons of non-ferrous ores, compared to 2.8 for CN.

(John Riddell)

CP 376199 GS
series 376190-376499

▼ This is one of 189 steel ore cars with five drop bottom doors on each side. It has a capacity of 1220 cubic feet and inside length of 25'-11" and height of 5'. It was built by Hawker-Siddeley Trenton Works in 1967. CP transports ore and concentrates from Sudbury-area INCO mines to the large smelter of INCO at Copper Cliff, from Falconbridge Nickel mines to their smelter. INCO and Falconbridge have their own rail lines but use CP ore cars. #376199 is shown at Levack Ontario in August 1979 near INCO's Levack Mine.

(Gary R. Zuters)

CP 375837 GT series 375800-375899

▲This is one of 100 Hart-Otis design cars built September 1929. It has an inside length 25'-11", flat bottom with five drop-bottom doors on each side and a capacity of 1180 cubic feet. In June 1932 CP had 967 ore cars and in January 1977, 1,100. CP uses ore cars in southern B.C. and the Sudbury area of Ontario, which is Canada's most important mining area. #376837 was shot in Whitefish Ontario in October 1978. These cars were used for shipping nickel ore from numerous mines around Sudbury to the large International Nickel Company of Canada (INCO) smelter at Copper Cliff, Ontario. *(John Riddell)*

CP 376668 GS series 376500-376846

◀Iron is a byproduct of processing nickel-iron-copper-sulphide ores. Side and end extensions of 18" were applied to 106 ore cars to ship less-dense iron ore pellets from the iron recovery mill at INCO's Copper Cliff smelter 80 miles to the Lake Huron harbour at Little Current. The extensions increased the interior height to 6'6" and the capacity from 1230 to 1524 cubic feet. The car has five drop bottom doors on each side and was built by Canadian Car and Foundry in 1926. Agincourt Yard, Toronto. November 1981. *(John Riddell)*

CP 375577 GS series 375500-375699

▼Photographed in Sudbury in August 1979, #375577 was painted in CP Rail scheme nine months earlier. This is one of 200 all-welded ore cars built by Hawker-Siddeley in December 1970. It has a flat bottom with drop-bottom doors on each side. It has a capacity of 1304 cubic feet and an interior length of 25'-11". The Sudbury area is the world's largest single source of nickel and is also Canada's largest copper source. *(Gary R. Zuters)*

CP 377238 HMA
377200-377249

◀ CP had 250 hopper-bottom cars built 1952 by Eastern Car Company in Trenton, Nova Scotia for handling lead-zinc ores and concentrates in the Tadanac B.C. area. #377238 has a capacity of 1400 cubic feet or 70 tons. It has a hopper bottom for self-clearing contents between the rails. The exterior length over strikers is 27'-2" and height is 11'-9". A batch of 48 cars have 9" side extensions to increase capacity for a higher volume of ore pellets which are less dense. CP had a total of 233 cars of this type in October 1970. These cars were originally black with 9" gothic lettering, then script and finally CP Rail lettering as shown. Nelson B.C. May 27 1980.
(Gary R. Zuters)

CP ore cars - HMA

▼ In May 1969 two strings of 377000-series ore cars await loading at the ore crushing plant at the Sullivan Mine of the Consolidated Mining and Smelting Company (COMINCO) at Kimberley B.C. The 45 visible cars carry script lettering with the two closest having been recently painted. When loaded, the cars will be routed to the COMINCO smelter at Trail B.C. COMINCO is a CP subsidiary company. By 1937, the Sullivan was the world's largest zinc-lead-silver mine, producing 10% of the world's output. *(John Riddell)*

 Gondolas

HIGH-SIDE

CP 351214 GS series 350000-351224
▲One of 1,225 cars, #351214 was built February 1930 by Canadian Car and Foundry Co. This is the 'Big Otis' composite coal gon. The Hart-Otis Company patented a mechanism of rolling shafts, chains and levers for opening and closing the drop doors in the flat bottom. It has an inside length of 41'6", a length over corner posts of 44'4" and a capacity of 2621 cubic feet. The car was painted in Winnipeg four months before this photo in Revelstoke, British Columbia, June 1967. *(Jim Parker)*

CP ? GS series 350000-351224
▲Built in 1926 this 'Big Otis' is awaiting scrapping in June 1969 at Ogden Shops, Calgary, Alberta. Faint lettering in the center of the car states FOR PORT MOODY COAL SERVICE ONLY. These cars were commonly used for coal service from Crowsnest Pass coal mines at Coleman, Blairmore, Natal and Michel to Port Moody, B.C. and to Fort William, Ontario. *(John Riddell)*

CP 352065 GS series 352000-352169
▼CP 352065 was built in March 1936. It has a capacity of 70 ton and 2600 cubic feet capacity. The inside length is 37'-6". It is shown awaiting scrapping at Ogden Shops, Calgary Alberta in January 1970. *(John Riddell)*

CP 352053 GS series 352000-352169

▲One of 170 composite coal cars built in 1936 by National Steel Car Co. in Hamilton Ontario as an improvement over the earlier 'Big Otis' coal gons. This was the first series of these cars. It has Yost drop bottom doors that side-discharge. It has a capacity of 70 ton and 2600 cubic feet capacity. The inside length is 37'-6". The white line indicates the load limit for gravel and ballast. Canmore, Alberta. May 1976. *(John Riddell)*

CP 348889 GS series 348850-349049

▼Built in 1958 by National Steel Car Co., CP 348889 has a capacity of 2670 cu. ft. or 70 tons. It has a length over strikers of 40'-9" and a 7' inside height. It has 3/3 corrugated ends and a flat bottom with 14 counter-balanced manually-operated drop-bottom doors hinged along the center of the car for dumping the contents outside the rails. The doors could be operated individually. Canmore, Alberta. May 1976. *(John Riddell)*

CP 348320 GS series 348000-348849

▼This is one of 850 70-ton high-side gons built in 1947 and 1948 by Eastern Car Co. of Trenton, Nova Scotia. This is a drop-bottom gondola with a flat bottom with 14 drop-bottom corrugated doors - seven per side. The doors are secured by Wine locks. The inside height is 7' and capacity is 2670 cu. ft. Canmore, Alberta. April 1974. *(John Riddell)*

CP 348962 GS series 348850-349049
◀ Some of the surviving drop-bottom hoppers received the CP Rail paint. This car has 14 counter-balanced manually operated drop-bottom doors hinged along the center of the car for dropping the contents outside of the rails. Doors can be opened individually. This series was built in 1958 by Eastern Car Company and has a capacity of 2670 cu. ft. The white line indicates the limit for gravel, sand and crushed stone. Toronto, October 3, 1987.
(John Riddell)

CP 348968 GS series 348850-349049
▲ Steel coal gon #348968 is in its natural habitat at the coke ovens in Michel B.C. in the Crowsnest Pass in June 1981. The 3/3 dreadnaught ends show clearly. The car was built in 1958 by the Eastern Car Company, Trenton, Nova Scotia and has a capacity of 2670 cu. ft. *(Robert Turner)*

CP 352991 GS series 352924-352998
◀ This is one of 75 drop-bottom gondolas built in 1963 for gypsum ore service on the Dominion Atlantic Railway, a CP subsidiary. Unit trains of 25 of these cars carry ore 12 miles from the Canadian Gypsum Company mine at Mantua to tidewater at Hantsport, Nova Scotia. The car has a capacity of 1925 cu. ft. or 70-tons, an inside height of 8'-3" and length over strikers of 40'-11". It has fixed sloping ends and drop-bottom doors hinged along center of car for dumping contents outside the rails. The doors are released manually and closed by compressed air. The cars were delivered in black with 9" lettering. August, 1978, Hantsport Nova Scotia. *(David P. Stremes)*

GONDOLAS

CP 362222 MWB series 362000-362499
▲This is one of 500 Hart Convertible ballast cars built in May 1912 by Canadian Car and Foundry in Turcot, Quebec, under license from the Hart-Otis Car Company of Montreal. It is steel with seven doors per side and wood ends and has a capacity of 1085 cu. ft. Barker's Point, New Brunswick. October 1, 1964. *(James O'Donnell)*

CP 362238 MWB series 362000-362499
▼Built in July 1912, this Hart Convertible gon still has its original K triple brakes. It has an inside height of 3'-7", inside length of 35'-3" and capacity of 1177 cubic feet. Lambton Shops, Toronto. April 1977. *(John Riddell)*

CP 369023 MWB series 368547-369775
▼CP 369023 was built in June 1912 as one of 612 ballast cars in series 368545-369775 (odd numbers only). It has an inside length of 30'-6", inside height of 3'-7" and a capacity of 969 cubic feet. It is shown in fresh paint, with its original arch bar trucks and K brakes in North Bay, Ontario in September 1955. *(Jim Parker)*

CP 338206 GD series 338100-338299
▲Built by Canadian Car and Foundry in June 1929, CP called these 200 gondolas 'stone cars' and commonly used them for ballast service. The car consisted of a steel underframe with a fishbelly center sill with a superstructure of 3' high wood sides and ends. The length over end sills was 41'8". It had a capacity of 995 cubic feet. A 2'2" steel door was in the center of each side. Stake pockets were attached to the outside of wood sides. Calgary, Alberta. July 1970. *(John Riddell)*

CP 340222 GB series 340200-340998
▼Built in 1952 by Eastern Car Company, this steel gon has an 3'-6" inside height and a 52'6" inside length. It has ribs of angle steel and a capacity of 1746 cu. ft. It carries the CP Rail red scheme. Kentville, Nova Scotia. June 1980. *(Gary Ness)*

CP 340642 GB series 340200-340998

▲This gon retains its original 1952 black paint with white lettering when seen in Calgary, Alberta in December 1974. It has an inside height of 3'-6", inside length of 52'-6" and capacity of 1746 cu. ft. *(John Riddell)*

CP 341998 GB series 341500-342399

▲Built in July 1957 by Eastern Car, this gon has rounded hat-section ribs. It has an inside length of 52'-6", inside height of 3'-6" and capacity of 1746 cu. ft. with a wood floor and drop-ends to accomodate loads longer than 52'6". Agincourt Yard, Toronto. April 1, 1989. *(John Riddell)*

CP 341232 GB series 341000-341499

▼Built in 1954 by Eastern Car, #341232 has angle ribs, a 52'-6" inside length and a 4'-0" inside height and capacity of 1996 cu. ft. Agincourt Yard, Toronto. January 21, 1989. *(John Riddell)*

CP 344395 GBSR series 344350-344399
▲This covered coil car has two cushion cradles for coils of sheet steel. It has three covers that can be removed individually and stacked on each other on the ground. It accomodates coils of 30" to 84" outside diameter. It has 36" diameter wheels, inside length of 52'-6" and height of 7'-8" and capacity of 1746 cu. ft. It was built in 1969 by Hawker-Siddeley. Toronto, Ontario. May 22, 1993. *(Gary R. Zuters)*

CP 344512 GBSR series 344500-344519
▼This covered gon is for shipping high-quality sheet steel, aluminum, tin, and nickel. The three-section roof has a round hatches at diagonal corners of cover. It has fixed ends and a moveable bulkhead. The inside length is 52'-0" and height is 5'-0". It has 36" diameter wheels, a capacity of 2361 cu. ft. and was built in 1966 by Hawker-Siddeley and numbered in 344200's. Toronto, Ontario. April 1, 1991. *(Gary R. Zuters)*

CP 336783 GB series 336700-336799
▲Built in November 1965, this gon has a 65'-6" inside length, 5'-0" inside height and 9'-7" width. It has 36" wheels in roller-bearing trucks, collapsible stake pockets and a nailable steel floor. Capacity is 3155 cu. ft. Leaside Yard, Toronto. June 27, 1992. *(John Slean)*

CP 336884 GB series 336800-336899
▲These mill gons are 1'-9" narrower than general gons to enable them to negotiate very sharp mill trackage and still remain within the plate B clearance dimensions. Built in 1958, this mill gon with drop ends, has a 65'-6" inside length, narrow 7'-9" inside width, 3'-6" inside height. It has 33" wheels and a capacity of 1776 cu. ft. Leaside Yard, Toronto. February 1981. *(Ken Grist)*

CP 337061 GB series 337000-337099
▼Built in 1962, this mill gon has inside length, width and height of 65'-6", 7'-9", 5'-0". It has drop ends and 33" wheels. Some of these gons were repainted in CP Rail Action Red. Capacity is 2538 cu. ft. Toronto, June, 1980. *(Ken Grist)*

WOOD CHIP CARS

CP 358062 HT series 358000-358599
▲ This is one of 20 triple-hoppers rebuilt at Angus shops - this one only two months earlier in July 1978 - with 4'-6" extensions to raise the capacity to 4521 cubic feet. The white panel states for WOOD CHIPS SERVICE DAR POINTS, meaning its restricted to the CP subsidiary Dominion Atlantic Railway. Interestingly, this car has been painted in script lettering some nine years after the CP Rail scheme was introduced. It was originally built by Eastern Car in 1947. Agincourt Yard, Toronto. September 3, 1978.
(Gary R. Zuters)

CP 343085 GTS series 343000-343099
▲ This woodchip gon, built in 1960, was converted from series 330000-330649 gons. It has an overall height of 14'-9" providing a capacity of 5466 cubic feet. The extensions were added in two stages with the higher extension added in April 1964. It has a full end-door on one end. Penticton, British Columbia. September 25, 1980. *(David Stremes)*

CP 343572 GTS series 343549-343599
▼ This car is one of 50 converted in 1964 from a 330000-series gons. It has an inside length of 52'-6" and inside height of 10'-9". It has a full end-door, a side-door and a capacity of 5313 cu. ft. Prince Albert, Saskatchewan. September 25, 1976. *(Ronald Plazzotta)*

CP 343630 GTS series 343600-343739
▲Forty gons were rebuilt in 1971 to carry wood chips in solid trains from Meadow Lake, Saskatchewan to the Prince Albert Pulp Co. Ltd. at Prince Albert. The service started in April 1972. Seven foot side extentions and a new full end-door for end unloading were added. It was rebuilt from a 330000-series gon and carries its rebuilt CP Rail Action Red paint. Capacity is 5412 cu. ft. Prince Albert, Saskatchewan. August 10, 1983. *(Ronald Plazzotta)*

CP 343404 GTS series 343400-343499
▼This 70 ton woodchip gon was built in 1969. It is 66'-4" long over strikers and has an inside height of 10'-8" providing a capacity of 6500 cubic feet. White River, Ontario. September 1979. *(Gary R. Zuters)*

CP 269941 LPS series 268803-269970
▶This is one of 52 boxcars without roofs and with extensions for wood chip service. It was assigned to the Atlantic Region and restricted to international and U.S. domestic service. It was loaded from the top or through the side doors by means of pneumatic or mechanical conveyors. It was unloaded from the side using front end loaders or pneumatic chip diggers. Originally the cars were built by Pullman-Standard in 1953-1954 as welded PS-1 boxcars. The inside height is 12'-4" and capacity is 4586 cu. ft. Brownville, Maine. May 1972.
(Jim Parker)

BATHTUB GONS

CP 349800 GT series 349800-349819
▲ This new bathtub gon was photographed in Agincourt Yard, Toronto on December 26, 1976 on its way west. This is a rotary-dump solid-bottom gondola designed for CP Rail unit coal train service from open-pit coal mines in the Rockies to the Roberts Bank marine terminal near Vancouver. It is unpainted aluminum and has a capacity of 4600 cu ft. and 105 tons. With its extreme light weight, the car is able to carry five times its weight in coal. The design features tapered sides and ends and a rounded bottom to permit free flow of coal during unloading, minimize the amount of residue remaining in car and lower the center of gravity (81 in. loaded). The designer, Mr. Teoli, retained the rights to the design and subsequently licensed the design and name 'bathtub' to the Youngstown Steel Door Company (now YSD Industries). YSD modified and sublicensed the design to other builders, such as Berwick and ACF. YSD later sold the rights to the Thrall Car Company. U.S.-built cars are shorter to accommodate shorter car dumpers. *(Gary R. Zuters)*

CP 799665 GT series 799623-799999
▲ Built by National Steel Car this new bathtub gon has a capacity of 4400 cu. ft. and 100 tons. It is seen in Agincourt Yard, Toronto on August 13, 1978. A rotary coupler is on the B-end to enable each car in a train to be rotated for dumping without uncoupling. All CP bathtub gons have a length of 55'-11' over strikers for compatibility with the rotary car dumpers. The car heights vary from 11-8 to 13-1. CP bought its first bathtub gons in 1969. The gons are also used in unit sulphur trains from natural gas plants in Alberta to the Vancouver Harbour. In January 1996, CP had 2,368 cars in nine series - 1,380 built by National Steel Car and 988 by Hawker Siddeley. *(Gary R. Zuters)*

CP 350822 GT series 350796-350867
◀ Photographed new on November 12, 1988 in Agincourt Yard, Toronto, CP 350822 carries a white panel to indicate that this car has a rotary coupler on each end so that it may be dumped while coupled to mid-train motive power. The car, with capacity of 4400 cubic feet, was built by National Steel Car in Hamilton, Ontario. The first unit coal train of 88 cars of coking coal destined for Japan arrived at Roberts Bank superport on April 30, 1970 after the 700-mile run from Sparwood, B.C. On September 14, 1978, CP Rail started 105-car unit coal trains from Corbin B.C. to Thunder Bay, Ontario for Ontario Hydro. The 2,600 mile round trip takes six days. *(Gary R. Zuters)*

 Flat Cars

CP 307694 FM series 307500-307971
▲This flat was built in September 1924. It has 13 side and 4 end stake pockets and a steel fishbelly center-sill. It has a drop-shaft brake wheel and KC air brakes. The length over strikers is 42'-6". The car carries typical flatcar lettering. Smiths Falls, Ontario. 1965. *(David Stremes)*

CP 301308 FM series 301300-301399
▼This steel flat was built in 1952. It has 15 stake pockets, a drop-shaft brake wheel and is 53'-1" long over strikers. Quebec Street Yard, London, Ontario. April 20, 1987. *(Don McQueen)*

CP 307401 FM series 307100-307499
▲This steel flat was built by Angus Shops in June 1919 as series 335500-335499. When built these had arch-bar trucks. It has fishbelly side-sills, 13 side and 4 end stake pockets and a length of 41'-8". The capacity is 102,000 pounds. It has a lever hand-brake control and KC air brakes. It is standard black with white lettering. Calgary, Alberta. *(Bryan Sirman)*

CP 315044 FM series 315000-315134
▼CP 315044 and 315091, carrying a load of twelve 100' poles, are 61' welded flat cars built in May 1967 by Napanee Industries Limited at Napanee, Ontario. Smiths Falls, Ontario. June 1969. *(Tom Hood)*

CP 315536 FC series 315500-315599
▲This is one of 100 general service flats built in 1981. It has a length over strikers of 90'-2" and 22 side stake pockets. The truck centers are spaced at 64'0". It carries standard CP Rail paint and lettering for flat cars. Oshawa, Ontario. January 1990. *(Michael Wearing)*

CP 301227 FMS series 301206-301733
▼This is one of 44 pulp wood cars fitted with 12 permanent steel stakes with load binder chains to connect the tops of opposite stakes. It has 15 stake pockets and was built in 1950. It has a fishbelly center sill and is 53'-1" over strikers. It carries the CP Rail paint scheme for flat cars. Thunder Bay, Ontario. September 1979. *(Gary Zuters)*

CP 309927 FD series 309925-309929
▼Built by General Steel Castings in 1930, depressed-center flat 309927 has a length over strikers of 56'-11" and a length of depression of 22'-7". It has a one-piece cast-steel Commonwealth underframe, a hand brake at each end and 30" diameter wheels in two 6-wheel trucks. The flat has a light weight of 108,000 pounds and a load capacity of 201,000 pounds. In 1956 CP had 16 depressed-center flats of three sizes. Agincourt Yard, Toronto. June 12, 1993. *(John Riddell)*

LOG CARS

CP 308430 FL series 308266-308500
▲ This is one of 200 skeleton log cars built in 1930 in Victoria for CP subsidiary Equimalt and Nanaimo Railway as 1000-1199. They were 43'-11" long with a 30" X 10" timber sill and painted black with white lettering. They served their entire lives on Vancouver Island moving logs from the forest to the log dumps at tidewater. The car still has its original arch-bar trucks when seen in Esquimalt, British Columbia in August 1969. At least some of these cars still retained their E&N lettering in 1946. *(John Riddell)*

CP 306059 FM series 306000-306249
▼ This is one of 250 40-ton log flat cars. It is a standard CP steel-frame flat with fishbelly center-sill, 13 stake pockets and log bunks on its deck. It is at Duncan, British Columbia, in June 1967 likely en route from Cowichan Lake to the log dump on Osborn Bay at Crofton. This car, built in April 1924 as series 335800-335945, was still in revenue service in June 1979. *(Jim Parker)*

STAKE CARS

CP 305572 FL series 305560-305609
▲This is one of 25 stake cars with 8 permanent stakes and 4 chain binders for poles. It has a length of 62'-9" and is loaded with new power poles at Aurora, Ontario in April 1979. It was built by National Steel Car in 1968. *(Gary R. Zuters)*

CP 305585 FL series 305560-305609
▼This stake car was built by National Steel Car in September 1968. It is less than a year old when shown at Smiths Falls, Ontario on August 1969. It is black with white lettering. Some of these cars received the CP Rail red scheme. *(Tom Hood)*

BULKHEAD FLAT CARS

CP 405003 LP Ex-series 32000-32088
▲This pulpwood bulkhead flatcar has a 41'0" inside length and a 7'8" bulkhead height. It is shown in company service loaded with new ties but was were designed for pulpwood service with open grid flooring that slopes down from the sides to the center of the car. In 1950, CP carried 1.4 million tons of pulpwood. Toronto, Ontario. June 12, 1993. *(John Riddell)*

CP 304073 FB series 304000-304199
▼Photographed at Butler, Wisconsin on July 13, 1990, CP 304073 is one of 200 lumber service flats built in 1965. It has a 51'6" inside length and 8'-6" high bulkheads. It has chain boxes on its left side for the tie-down chains and ratchet load binders on its right side. *(Ronald Plazzotta)*

CP 304576 FB series 304401-304651
▲CP 304576 is one of 250 bulkhead flats built in 1969 and used in the Eastern Region for shipping pulpwood to pulp and paper mills. It is designed for longitudinal loading of pulpwood with a 51'6" inside length and 10' high bulkheads. It has six pairs of permanently mounted 10' side stakes per side. Opposing stakes are connected by chain tie downs across the top of the load. 13 stake pockets are along centerline of the floor. Thunder Bay, Ontario. May 16, 1980. *(Gary R. Zuters)*

CPI 317138 FB series 317000-317199
▼Photographed in Agincourt Yard, Toronto in February 1988, CPI 317138 is five months old. It has a 66'-0" inside length and 10'10" bulkheads. Reporting mark CPI indicates it is restricted to international service only and is not to be loaded for domestic points. The car was built by Marine Industries Limited and leased by CP Rail from North American Car. CP purchased the car after 1989. *(Mike Wearing)*

CP 318245 FBS series 318000-318283
▼This center-beam flat was built in May 1988 by National Steel Car for the Canadian General Transit Company (CGTX) who leases it to CP Rail. The length between bulkheads is 73'-0". Agincourt Yard, Toronto. February 3, 1989. *(John Slean)*

TOFC

CP 320 trailer
▲Two unidentifiable CP double-hitch flat cars are each loaded with two green CP highway semi-trailers of 24' or 26' length. The nearest trailer has yellow script lettering while the far trailer has yellow block lettering. A CP steam locomotive is stored on the right. London, Ontario. August 1957. *(Jim Parker)*

CP 503201 FC
series 503002-503851
◀This 46' flat car was built in 1958 by National Steel Car using a design of the National Research Council. It is equipped with an ACF hydraulic hitch and designed for end-loading of single highway semi-trailers up to 42' long. Ten such cars were fitted for passenger service. The hitch is at the A-end and safety posts are on the car sides in line with the hitch. These posts were removed in January 1974. At the right, the brake stand is mounted on the car side. Toronto, Ontario. April 1968.
(Jim Parker)

CP 505987 FC
series 505965-505999
◀CP 505987 is one of 35 54' flat cars equipped with an ACF hydraulic hitch and designed for end-loading of single highway semi-trailers up to 45' long. The trailer was built in 1966 by Canadian Trailmobile Limited in Scarborough Ontario, a subsidiary of National Steel Car. Smith Transport later became part of CP Transport. Smiths Falls, Ontario. February 1973. *(Tom Hood)*

CP 678 Trailer
▲This smooth side, side door trailer was photographed at the John Street piggyback terminal in downtown Toronto in September 1960. In January 1985, CP owned 766 trailers of 23 types. *(Jim Parker)*

**CP 504484 FC
series 504000-504649**
▶Built by Marine Industries Ltd. in August 1975, CP 504484 with an inside length of 54'-4" for end-loading of trailers up to 45' long. Container CPPU 260952 of length 44'-3", one of 195, is loaded on chassis CPPZ 165418, one of 220. As of January 1985, end-loading ramps were located at 28 locations on the CP system. Edmonton, Alberta. August 19, 1983. *(Ronald Plazzotta)*

CP 507000 FC series 507000-507009
▼One of ten CP four-wheel flat cars built in April 1961 by General Motors Diesel Limited in London, Ontario. The car was designed by GMDL to meet a concept outlined by CP and Smith Transport. The light-weight container flats could be loaded from either side by any side-loading device. At one end of the car was a standard ACF trailer hitch which locked onto the trailer body kingpin. At the other end of the car was a rear guide-frame which positioned and supported the container as the tandem wheel assembly does when the unit is in highway service. The external length was 46'-10". The cars, called 'Portager', were off the CP roster by 1977. Photographed on the GMDL test track in April 1961. An article on these cars was published in the April-May 1977 issues of *TRAINS* magazine. In the background is a new GMDH1 diesel for the Electric Reduction Co.
(Don McQueen Collection)

AUTO RACKS

CP 550047 FA series 550000-550384
▲This tri-level open autorack is one of a series of 385. It has a length of 89'-1". #550047 was built in 1963 - the deck by National Steel Car and the tri-level rack by Whitehead & Kales. Toronto, Ontario. May 8, 1988. *(Gary Zuters)*

CP 556112 FA series 556100-556139
▼This is one of 40 tri-level enclosed autoracks built by National Steel Car - the deck in 1976 and the rack in December 1983. It has 10" end-of-car cushioning. Deck one is 5'2" high, deck two is 5'1" and the inside length is 89'4". Toronto, Ontario. March 2, 1984. *(Gary Zuters)*

CP 540109 FA series 540000-540149
▼This bi-level open autorack, built 1965, is for autos and trucks. The second deck is 6'11" high. Toronto, Ontario. November 20, 1987. *(Gary Zuters)*

CONTAINER FLATS

CP 520025 FC series 520025-520030
▲In 1965 CP built six 83'2" container flat cars from retired heavyweight passenger cars. They were commonly coupled to the end of passenger trains between Montreal and Toronto. This one is at Smiths Falls, Ontario in December 1971. These flats were gone by 1977. *(Tom Hood)*

CP 521135 LF series 521050-521249
▼This 81' container flat has special bolsters for overhead loading of two 40' or four 20' international intermodal containers. Two transverse bolsters for 20' containers fold down out of the way to accomodate 40' containers. The deckless flat has a 100 ton capacity and is equipped with end-of-car cushioning. It was built by Hawker-Siddeley Trenton in 1975. London, Ontario. August 1977.
(John Allen, Don McQueen Collection)

CP 522527 FC series 522506-522770
▼This 46' container flat, built May 1984, will carry one 40' international or 44'-3" domestic container. Container CPPU 260764 is 44'3" and has a capacity of 60,000 pounds. As of January 1985, CP owned 2,000 containers of 18 types and had container handling equipment located at 17 locations system-wide. Winnipeg, Manitoba. October 1984. *(F. Headon)*

CP 524103 FM series 524100-524269

▲This new three-pack of double-stack container flats, built by National Steel Car, is seen in Toronto on November 15, 1992. Each car has a 48'1" well length and the overall coupled length is 212'4". It has Plate H clearance. To transport double-stacked 2.9 metre containers from coast to coast, CP undertook a $15 million project to enlarge tunnels and snowsheds between Vancouver and Montreal-Toronto. In 1984 CP had 85 tunnels. *(Gary. R. Zuters)*

CP 524000-524001-524002 FM

▼Although CP was early with single-stack container cars it did not quickly commit to the double-stack container trend of North American railroads, likely due to numerous low clearance restrictions such as the tunnel between Windsor and Detroit. These new 3-unit double-stack cars, shown at Toronto on November 17, 1991, were the first owned by CP and were used to test double-stack operation between Montreal and Toronto and the terminal handling of containers. Each car has a 40' well length and a Plate 'F-Plus' clearance. CP also leased 50 well-type cars from TTX Inc. and started regular service on trains 928 and 929 in June 1992. *(Gary Zuters)*

COIL CARS

CP 313531 FMS series 313500-313549
▲Built in 1966 under license by International Equipment Co., Napanee, Ontario, #313531 is one of fifty 100-ton Evans-design cars for carrying coiled sheet steel. It is equipped with two wood-lined troughs with adjustable crossbars, two removeable steel covers and a Hydra-Cushion underframe with 20" travel. The left red cover carries the CP Rail paint while the black right cover carries the older script lettering. Toronto. April 6, 1990. *(Gary Zuters)*

CP 313515 FMS series 313500-313549
▼These coil cars have a 48' interior length and a 55'-0" length over strikers. The car has two 22'-1" long loading troughs, separated by a partition. Adjustable crossbars prevent longitudinal movement of coils in the troughs during shipping. The CP cars have no side running boards which are common on other coil cars. Brackets are attached on the top of each cover to enable the covers to be stacked on the ground when removed. The car can accomodate steel coils of 30" to 84" outside diameter. The wheels are 36" diameter. #313515 was built in March 1967. Toronto. July 18, 1990. *(Gary Zuters)*

CP 313542 FMS series 313500-313549
▼This coil car was repainted one month earlier in CP Action red without the multi-mark. Starting in 1988, CP stopped applying the multi-mark when repainting cars. Toronto, Ontario. November 1988. *(Gary Zuters)*

 ## Cabooses

CP 437040

▲This traditional CP wood caboose is freshly painted with yellow hand rails. It has a steel underframe and is 34'10" over strikers. CP preferred the word caboose however the word van was also commonly used. The 1985 CP Rail equipment roster uses the word van. The word van originated from the British term guard's van. North Bay, Ontario. Circa 1940. *(B.F. Cutler, Keith Sirman Collection)*

CP 436995 - series 436980-437004

▼This classic CP wood caboose has mineral red sides, platforms, trucks and bright red ends on the body and cupola. The roof is black and the handrails yellow. It carries 9" lettering and 6" numerals. The cupola has been sheathed in metal and has a sliding screen on the window. The storm door is latched in the open position. Built in 1941 by CP Angus shops, it has a steel underframe and is 34'-10" over strikers. It was scrapped before 1965. Windsor, Ontario. March 1962.
(Emery J. Gulash)

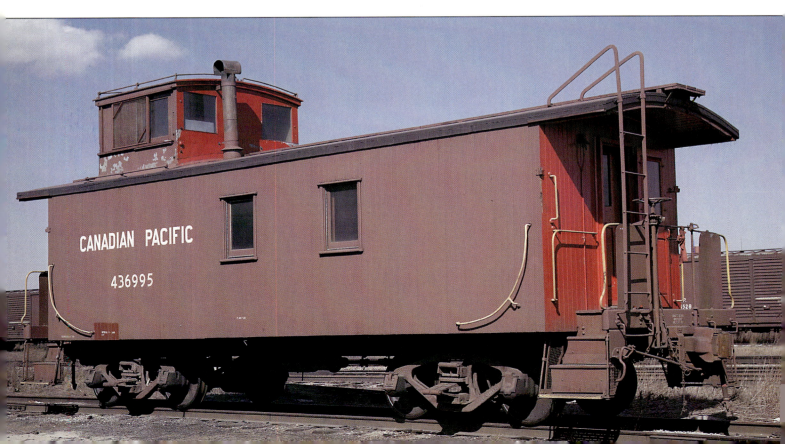

CP 435471
▲This view of a steel underframe wood caboose with arch bar trucks, shows its black roof. CP cabooses originally had 10 windows in their cupolas - three in each end and two in each side. In the 1930's, the center end windows and one on each side were blocked, likely to reduce the sun heating the cupola. Toronto, Ontario. August 1956. *(Jim Parker)*

CP 435472
▼This 35'5" wood underframe caboose has arch bar trucks and K brakes. It was scrapped before 1965. Cabooses with wood underframes were either rebuilt with steel underframes or scrapped. In 1947, 1,230 cabooses were in service, 217 with wood underframes. While similiar in appearance, CP wood cabooses were of four lengths over strikers: 24'10", 34'10", 35'5" and 39'5". In 1947, the number of each length in service was 2, 248, 963 and 17 respectively. Windsor, Ontario. March 1962. *(Emery J. Gulash)*

CP 437073
▲CP 437073 was on a prairie mixed train when photographed in Swift Current, Saskatchewan on October 4, 1959. This was one of 255 such cabooses in service in 1956. It has a steel underframe and K brakes. A red CP Express truck is in background. *(Lou Schmitz)*

CP 436729
▼This recently painted caboose shows the standard colors as new. It is a 30-ton steel-underframe caboose built in 1920. Until recent years each freight conductor was assigned his own caboose, home for the train crew while away from their terminal. In the last years of CP caboose usage, they were run through crew change points. CP wood cabooses were lit by kerosene lamps and had no toilet facilities. Approximately 70 such wood cabooses are preserved in museums and privately across Canada. Vancouver, B.C. October 29, 1960. *(Doug Cummings, Lou Schmitz Collection)*

CP 435415
▲Freshly painted #435415 was in Ottawa Ontario when photographed in 1957. It has a steel underframe and is 35'5" long over strikers. In 1956 CP numbered its 1,135 wood cabooses from 435018 to 437264. *(Graham Stremes)*

CP 435076
▼This is one of 502 steel underframe 30-ton cabooses in service in 1965. The length is 35'-5' over strikers and it retains its K brakes. The wood cupola is sheathed in metal and the paint is peeling. Most CP wood cabooses were originally built with three windows per side. During rebuilding, the windows farthest from the cupola were blocked out leaving only two on each side. It carries the script lettering which started to be applied in 1959. Windsor, Ontario. October 1965. *(Emery J. Gulash)*

CP 437110
▲This is one of two short CP cabooses used on the Rossland Subdivision in southern B.C. The other was #437111. It is 24'-10" over strikers and has a steel-underframe. Originally built 34'10" long in the 1930's, they were modified in 1944 by shortening by 10' to create short cabooses. They were identical to standard cabooses with 10' removed. A third short caboose, #437134, was used in Winnipeg yard service as late as 1962. Trail, B.C. July 24, 1973. *(Michael R. Wearing)*

CP 437110
◀CP 437110 is shown in Nelson B.C. in September 1974, recently painted mineral red with bright red ends and CP Rail lettering. Prior to these short cabooses, switch crews on Rossland Subdivision trains were without accomodation from the time the run to Warfield began in 1930. Since the switch engine pushed its train up the 3.9% grade, a switchman was required to ride the leading car. These short cabooses provided some protection although a crew member rode the platform prepared to stop the train if necessary. This brown color was unusual as standard caboose color in 1974 was CP Rail yellow. In January 1979, #437110 was plywood-sheathed at Angus Shops and painted yellow.
(Robert D. Turner)

CP 410392

▶ This yard caboose, restricted to the Calgary yard, was built from a wood boxcar with steel-reinforced ends. Each corner has steps, a door and a ladder. The caboose is shown awaiting scrapping at Ogden shops, Calgary in September 1968. Similiar cabooses #410398 and #410497 served in Winnipeg and Lethbridge yards respectively. *(John Riddell)*

CP 436725

▼ Two cabooses provide crew accomodation on a steam-powered maintenance-of-way work train in rural Manitoba on August 12, 1959. The near caboose #436725, built 1920, has a taller cupola than the far caboose.
(Jim Walder, John Riddell Collection)

CP 437312 series 437268-437404

▶ This is one of 137 steel cabooses built in 1948-49. It is 35'11" long over strikers and maintains the style of earlier CP wood cabooses. The storm door is latched in the open position. Fredericton, New Brunswick. 1971. *(Gordon Jomini)*

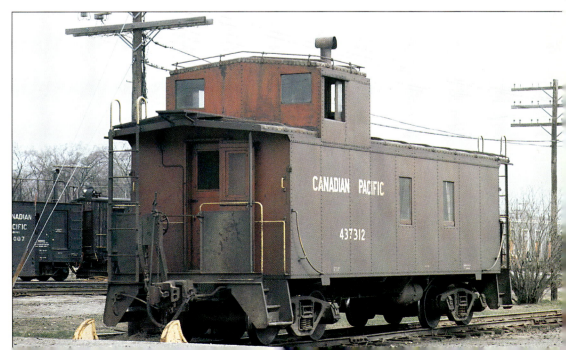

CP 438709 series 439706-439714
▲This steel caboose was new when photographed in Agincourt Yard, Toronto in January 1968. It is 37'8" long over strikers and includes an oil heater, electric stove and lighting and a toilet. It was later renumbered in September 1974 into series 434030-434071. *(Jim Parker)*

CP 437156
◀Built in 1941 by CP Angus shops, #437156 has been plywood sheathed and the plywood is delaminating showing bulges. It was painted at Angus shops in December 1971 with the red, yellow and black paint scheme that followed the mineral red. It has a steel underframe and AB brakes. Fredricton, New Brunswick. 1973.
(Gordon Jomini)

CP 438591
◀This wood caboose is shown in October 1977 in Agincourt Yard, Toronto after being recently painted in CP Rail colors. It has its number on the cupola. The 'T' in the circle indicates this caboose is allocated to transfer service. *(Gary R. Zuters)*

CP 437106
▲CP applied plywood sheathing over many wood sheathed cabooses. This plywood-sheathed caboose was built in April 1944 with a steel underframe and K brakes. Late CP cabooses differed little from the early truss-rod wood cars other than having steel underframe and blocked windows in sides and cupola. St. Boniface, Manitoba. July 1983. *(Emery J. Gulash)*

CP 434016 - series 434000-434029
▲Originally built in 1948 as series 438700-438717, this steel caboose was renumbered to #434016 in September 1974. Windsor, Ontario. July 1983.
(Emery J. Gulash)

CP 439075
▶This freshly painted steel caboose is shown in Fredericton, New Brunswick in 1973. One of the cupola windows has a frost shield. *(Gordon Jomini)*

STEEL, CENTER CUPOLA

CP 437500 series 437455-437504
▲Built by CP Angus shops in 1954, this is one of 50 such steel cabooses. It has a center cupola and is 33'2" over end sills. It is shown in Agincourt, Ontario in July 1964 in its original paint. A similar caboose, #437464, is preserved in Brockville, Ontario. *(Jim Parker)*

CP 437496 series 437455-437504
▼This steel caboose has been repainted with script lettering. It has brown sides, bright red ends and cupola ends, yellow safety appliances and a yellow metal grid walkway around its cupola. A railing protects the smoke jack on the roof. Fredericton, New Brunswick. 1970. *(Gordon Jomini)*

CP 437482 series 437455-437504
▲This was the final paint scheme applied to these steel cabooses. The running boards have been removed. Agincourt Yard, Toronto. July 8, 1987
(Gary R. Zuters)

CP 437265 series 437265-437267
▶This is one of three steel bay-window cabooses built in July 1948. It is shown in its original paint in Golden, B.C. in August 1970. The length over strikers is 36'-9". *(John Riddell)*

CP 437266 series 437265-437267
▼Script lettering has been applied to #437266 as shown in Regina, Saskatchewan in August 1973. In March 1969 it was renumbered 439057 and in 1989 again renumbered 437266. This caboose is preserved in a private collection south of Calgary.   *(Bryan Sirman, Keith Sirman Collection)*

CP 437265 series 437265-437267
◀ Repainted in the CP Rail scheme in Ogden Shops, December 1977, #437265 has been fitted with a fuel tank on its roof. It has yellow sides and ends and a black roof and underframe. Calgary, Alberta. September 24, 1979. *(Robert B. Hadlow, Gary Zuters Collection)*

CP 434604 series 434600-434615
▼ This is one of 16 extended-vision cabooses built by CP Angus shops in 1977. It is 43'-1" over strikers. It has an oil heater and electric stove. Approximately 466 similiar cabooses were built between 1968 and 1981. CP stopped using cabooses on mainline trains in approximately 1991. Agincourt Yard, Toronto. June 1978. *(Gary R, Zuters)*

CP 438851 series 438851-438860
◀ This is one of ten extended-vision cabooses built in 1969 and renumbered in 1974 to the 434000 series. Its running boards have been removed. In January 1985, CP Rail had 823 vans in service numbered 434000-439549 but by 1994 there were 298 on the roster, active or stored. Agincourt Yard, Toronto. November 1971. *(Jim Parker)*

 # Maintenance of Way

DUMP CARS

CP 455069 MWD series 455065-455099

▲On June 1, 1980, #455069 was in Smiths Falls, Ontario when photographed. It is one of 35 30-cubic yard two-way side-hinged air-dump cars built in 1931 by Canadian Car and Foundry using a design of the Magor Car Corporation. It has an inside length of 33'-2". *(David Stremes)*

CP 455172 MWD Series 455100-455224

▼This differential air-dump car was built in 1947 by National Steel Car. It has an inside length of 29'-6" and a 30 cubic yard capacity. It dumps by air to either side of the track. The door in the unloading side automatically folds down during the dumping operation and closes itself when the body returns to the central position. It is in its original black paint and white lettering. Leaside Yard, Toronto. November 1991. *(John Slean)*

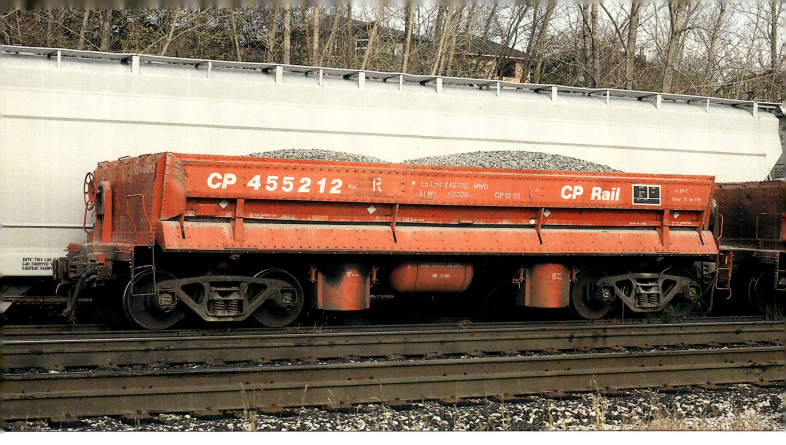

CP 455212 MWD Series 455100-455224
▲This air-dump car is one of 125 built in 1959 by National Steel Car in series 360400-360524. It has an inside length of 29'-6" and a 30 cubic yard capacity. It dumps by air to either side of the track. It carries CP Rail action red paint with white lettering. Leaside Yard, Toronto. November 1991. *(John Slean)*

CP 456194 MWB series 456000-456325
▼This is one of 325 ballast cars was built in July 1978 by the National Steel Car Co. under the Government of Canada funded Branchline Rehabilitation program. In the mid-1970's many branchlines required upgrading and these cars were built to implement that program. It has a capacity of 2200 cubic feet or 100 tons and four outlets fitted with Morrison-Knudson ballast gates. The roller bearing trucks have 36" wheels. The length over strikers is 41'-7" and the height is 11'-6". Leaside Yard, Toronto. November 3, 1991. *(John Slean)*

FLANGERS

**CP 400516 MWK
series 400416-400516**

▶ In January 1965 CP owned 25 single-track flangers such as #400516 which had been built in 1917. It has a wood body on a steel underframe and is 30'0" over end sills. The scoops are air-operated. The arch bar trucks are attached by chains to restrict their movement should they derail in snow. Flangers were painted like cabooses - freight car red with bright red ends. Penticton, B.C. April 1969.
(Stan Styles, John Riddell Collection)

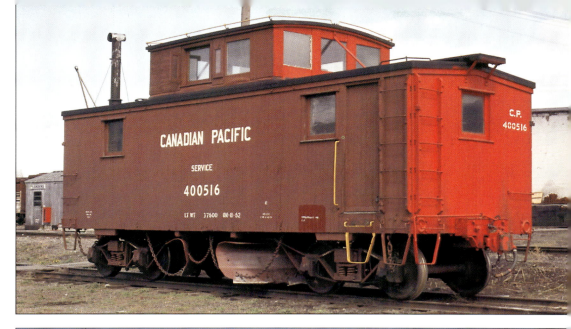

**CP 400491 MWK
series 400416-400516**

▶ This view shows script lettering scheme on a 1920-built flanger. A scoop mounted at each end of the car enables the flanger to be operated in either direction. It has K brakes with a vertical shaft for the hand brake. Sutherland, Saskatchewan. August 1972.
(Stan Styles, John Riddell Collection)

**CP 400404 MWK
series 400404-400405**

▼ This is one of two flangers built in 1963 from 1929-built radial-roof steel boxcars. Like the wood flangers it is boxcar red with bright red ends and script lettering Agincourt Yard, Toronto. October 12, 1981.
(John Riddell)

PLOWS

CP 400774 MWK
series 400761-400785

▲This typical CP steel single-track snow plow, built in 1925 by CP Angus shops, is equipped with air-operated hinged side wings and ice cutters. The width with the wings closed was 11'-0" and with wings extended was 16'-0". All air operation is controlled directly from the cupola. The length over all was 32'-0" and trucks were on 18'-0" centers. It has the standard plow colours of black with bright red ends and white gothic lettering. In 1956 CP owned 164 steel single-track plows. Smiths Falls, Ontario. February 2, 1992.
(Pierre Ozorak, Gary Zuters Collection)

CP 400632 MWK
series 400626-400785

◄ In July 1987, #400632 was at Whitewood, Saskatchewan when photographed. A safety hand rail is on the roof extending to the cupola. the height to the top of eave is 11'3" and cupola is 14'10" has an cook stove. It has white CP Rail lettering with black sides, roof and underbody, red ends and yellow safety appliances. This plow was built in April 1924.
(Emery J. Gulash)

CP 400794 MWK series 400788-400799
▲This steel plow is for clearing snow to the right on double-track. Double-track plows deflect snow to only one side. CP had both right-hand and left-hand steel plows. Built in September 1926 #400794 carries the standard gothic lettering. In January 1956, CP owned 27 steel double-track plows. Farnham, Quebec. November 11, 1975.
(Gary Zuters)

CP 400822 MWK series 400814-400824
▼This view shows the flush side of a right-hand double-track plow. It has a half-height wing on its left. Built in July 1914 it carries the script lettering. During off-seasons, plows are often stored with their windows boarded over. Agincourt Yard, Toronto. May 24, 1981. *(John Riddell)*

SPREADERS

CP 402842 MWE series 402800-402855
▲This is one of CP's Jordan 'standard' ballast-spreaders manufactured by the O.F. Jordan Company of East Chicago, IL. It does not have a cab for the operator. The wing blades are extended by pneumatic cylinders. It is black with white lettering. In 1956 CP owned 47 'standard' spreaders. A similar CP spreader is preserved in the West Coast Railway Heritage Park in Squamish B.C. Kamloops, British Columbia. August 1974.
(Stan Styles, David Stremes Collection)

CP 402852 MWE series 402800-402855
▼This view shows the front end of a Jordan 'standard' ballast-spreader with a wooden cab. Jordan spreaders are pushed by a locomotive at 4 or 5 mph with their wings extended to spread ballast to achieve a specific contour of ballast and roadbed. They are also used to clear snow. The pointed steel bars below the coupler are ice cutters. It carries script lettering. London, Ontario. October 1973. *(Emery J. Gulash)*

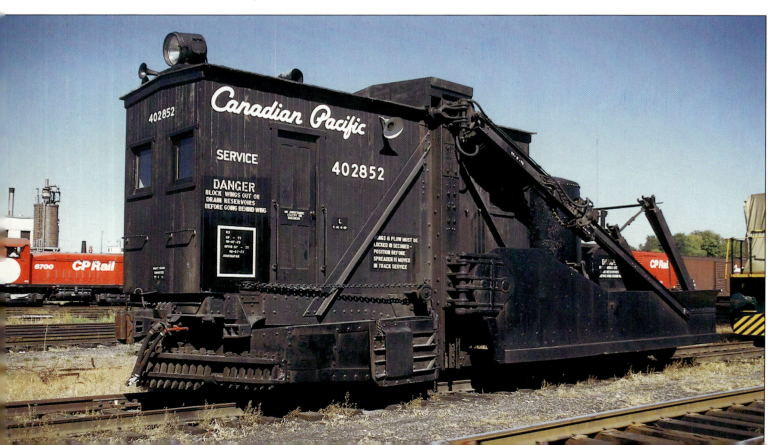

CP 402863 MWE
▲This Jordan Type 'A' ballast-spreader has a 6-foot wide wooden cab mounted back of the wing where the operator can observe the wing braces in operation. Built in 1931, this spreader weighs about 65 tons and is equipped with ice cutters along the lower edge of the front plow. The heater stack extending from the cab and the safety appliances are yellow. This is one of eight CP Type 'A' spreaders in 1965. Agincourt Yard, Toronto. June 1993. *(John Riddell)*

CP 402884 MWE
series 402882-402884
▶This Jordan hydraulic Type 'J' spreader ditcher has a modern glass greenhouse cab in front which is well suited for snowplow duty. The silver tank is for fuel oil for the cab heater during cold weather operation. The stove stack extends from the cab. It is freshly painted with script lettering. In January 1985, CP Rail owned 60 ballast spreaders and spreader ditchers of six types. Carberry, Manitoba. July, 1983. *(Emery J. Gulash)*

CP 410020 series 410005-410022
▶This is one of 11 boxcars in 1994 fitted with steel frames for icicle breaking service in the mountains west of Calgary. During freezing temperatures icicles that form in tunnels are a potential source of damage to high loads and passenger dome cars. These ice breaker cars are coupled behind the locomotives to knock down any icicles and avoid any damage. The stencil reads TO BE USED ONLY IN ICICLE BREAKING SERVICE WEST OF CALGARY - CAR CONTAINS BALLAST - DO NOT REMOVE. Originally 1959-built boxcar #56936, in 1988 it was converted to ice breaker #410013 and renumbered in 1993 to #410020. Field, B.C. April 1995.

(Robert Turner)

TANK CARS

CP 389593 T series 389471-389989

▲This tank car for CPR oil transport was built 1912 and retains its original K brakes. It has a capacity of 10,071 US gallons or 8,393 Imperial gallons. It awaits scrapping at Ogden shops, Calgary in December 1972. In January 1956 CP owned 117 such old tank cars in company service for oil and water. Similar tank cars were commonly used as auxilary water cars coupled to steam locomotive tenders on prairie freight trains. Apparently tank cars didn't wear out as rapidly like other types of freight cars. *(John Riddell)*

CP 400163 T series 400100-400215

▼CP 400163 is one of 125 tank cars for shipping company diesel oil. It has no steam coils for heating the contents. It has a capacity of 16,000 imperial gallons. a length over strikers of 51'-5" and 33" wheels. It is black with white gothic lettering. It was built in 1953 in series 389100-389224. These tank cars rarely if ever left the CP lines. Toronto, Ontario. September 16, 1985. *(Gary Zuters)*

SCALE TEST CARS

CP 420926 WT series 420925-420927
▲This scale test car built by Atlas Steel in June 1916 as #400926. It has a length over strikers 15'-3", roller bearing journals and a sealed weight of 60,000 pounds. Scale cars had only hand brakes and no air brakes to avoid brake-shoe wear which would cause a variation in their weight from that measured on the master scale. It is black with yellow grabs. In 1956 CP owned four scale test cars. Agincourt Yard, Toronto. May 28, 1977. *(Dave Whitnall, Gary Zuters Collection)*

CP 420925 and 420931 WT
▼Scale test cars were often operated in pairs so that the track scale could be calibrated at two different weights. CP 420925, built in 1916 by Atlas Steel as #400925, weighs 70,000 pounds and carries a small multimark. CP 420931, weighs 200,000 pounds and was built in 1982 from MLW booster unit B-100. It is black with white safety appliances. Manitoba. July 1983. *(Emery J. Gulash)*

CP 420928 WT
▲Built by Atlas Steel in January 1953 this car has a sealed weight of 80,000 pounds or 36288 kilograms. It is black with yellow end stripes, brake wheel and hand grabs. On the right is an orange CN scale car. Toronto, Ontario. October 8, 1984. *(Gary Zuters)*

CP 420934 WT
▼This scale test car with a sealed weight of 254,500 pounds was converted in May 1990 from 32' slurry covered hopper #381928 built October 1960. It is black with white railings. Winnipeg, Manitoba. February 1992. *(F. Headon)*

CRANES

CP 5603-01

▶ This freshly-painted CP Rail Burro crane is mounted on rails on 52'-6" flat car #402216. The crane boom is supported by a frame on the flat car. At the work site, the self-propelled Burro crane is usually removed from the flat car down a rail-ramp to the track. A small red multi-mark logo is on the side of the yellow crane. Sudbury, Ontario. October 1, 1979.
(Jim McRae)

CP 414326 MWW series 414322-414327

▲ This coal-fired steam-powered wreck crane weights 195,000 pounds and has a lifting capacity of 100 tons. Like most cranes in cold weather climates it has a wooden cab to provide protection for its operators. It was built by Industrial Works, Bay City, Michigan. The boom rests on a trolley on the coupled auxiliary car. The crane is black over-all with yellow safety appliances and hook and red window frames. Esquimalt, British Columbia. August 1975.
(John Riddell)

CP 414330 MWW series 414329-414341

▼ One of twelve 150-ton steam-powered wreck cranes with a weight of 195,000 pounds has a lifting capacity of 100 tons. A steel cab encloses the operator and the boom rests on a moveable trolley on the coupled auxiliary car. Built in 1913 by Industrial Works, it is preserved at the West Coast Railway Museum at Squamish B.C. It is black with red windows and yellow hook. In January 1956, CP owned 17 cranes, 61 wreck cranes and 4 derricks. Vancouver, British Columbia. September 22, 1980.
(David Stremes)

CP 414470 MWW series 414470-414480

▲This view shows the wreck train stationed at Sudbury, with one of CP's eleven 200-ton self-propelled diesel-powered wreck cranes. #414470 was built by Industrial Brownhoist as steam-powered and later converted to diesel operation. It has six-wheel trucks and is black with yellow safety appliances and hook. Auxiliary car #412569 is a cut-down single-sheathed boxcar and water car #415791 is a former steam locomotive tender. In January 1956, CP Rail owned 17 cranes, 61 wreck cranes and four derricks of various capacities. Sudbury, Ontario. April 1973. *(Jim McRae)*

CP 414501 MWW series 414500-414503

▲This is one of four CP Rail 250-ton self-propelled wreck cranes manufactured by Industrial Brownhoist. Its travelling speed is 2.3 mph. It was painted only four days earlier in the CP Rail scheme with yellow safety appliances and hooks. Built in 1946, #414501 is assigned as the Toronto Auxilary. Agincourt Yard, Toronto. September 24, 1987.

(Gary R. Zuters)

LE&N M-6

◀ This is a line car of the Lake Erie and Northern Railway - a CP subsidiary 75 mile electric railway in southern Ontario. Built from a 1934 Ford truck it was used for maintaining the overhead catenary when the 1500 volts DC overhead power was off. It is shown in April 1961 at the LE&N shops in Preston, Ontario, conspicuously painted in yellow with black stripes for maximum visibility while working on the line. It is preserved at the Halton County Radial Railway Museum at Rockwood, Ontario. A LE&N electric locomotive is in background. *(Emery J. Gulash)*

OUTFIT CARS

CP 410883 MWX
▲This Foreman & Tool Car was built from a 36' double-sheathed wood boxcar. It has steel ends, original arch bar trucks and K brakes, mismatched windows and a drip-strip above the door. Many cars typically had doors cut in their ends to allow crew passage between coupled cars. Ogden Shop scrap track, Calgary. December 1971. *(John Riddell)*

CP 403726 MWX
▲This Foreman & Tool Car was built from a 36' Fowler-patent single-sheathed boxcar. It has a metal roof and its original K brakes. Many work cars were made from these boxcars with a variety of window and door configurations. Calgary, Alberta. April 1974. *(John Riddell)*

CP 401532 MWM series 401518-401538
▼This is one of 17 Stores Department Supply cars built between 1910 and 1913 for company service. It is wood with radial roof and a length over strikers of 48'-8". The trucks are mis-matched. The standard CP colour for service house cars is brown with black roof. Ogden Shops scrap track, January 1969. *(John Riddell)*

CP 402488 MWT series 402004-402699

▶This wood tender flat for wreck crane #414326 has truss rods and a trolley supporting the end of the crane boom. The two long boxes contain tools. It is boxcar red with black roof. A photo of the crane is in the crane section. Esquimalt, British Columbia. August 1975. *(John Riddell)*

CP 403503 MWT

▼Tool Car 403503 was built from a double-sheathed wood box car with steel ends. The stencilled sign indicates FIRE FIGHTING EQUIPMENT KEPT IN THIS CAR. On its left is CP Rail & Tie Car #403544. On its right is a flatcar carrying trucks. In the left foreground is CP steel flat #312705 from series 312600-312724, built December 1919. It was converted from a former piggyback flat car and is used only as an idler under overhanging loads. The length over strikers is 41'-6". It is black with white lettering. The weathered flatcar on the right appears to have been used for logs. In the background are two wood cabooses with different height cupolas and the CP brick ten-stall roundhouse. Esquimalt, British Columbia. August 1975. *(John Riddell)*

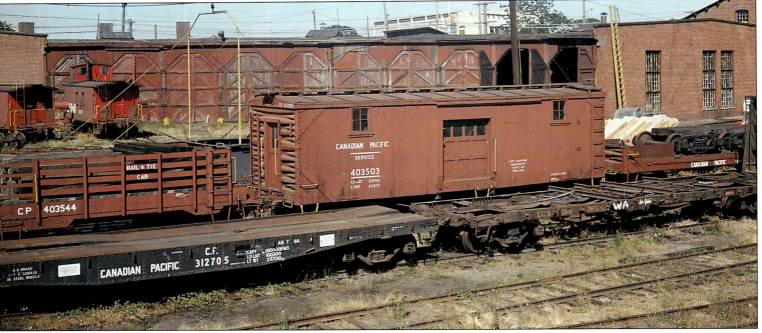

CP 412667 MWX

▼Many CP outfit cars were built from steel boxcars such as this one. This Sleeper Tool Car was formerly a 1929-built radial-roof boxcar. It has aluminum frame windows and a fuel tank mounted on the roof to supply two heaters whose stacks extend from the roof. It carries the script lettering. In January 1956, CP owned 5,551 pieces of rolling stock in company service. Winnipeg, Manitoba. September 21, 1995. *(F. Headon)*